M000082421

THE CARDS I WAS DEALT
DEALT
THE HAND THAT I
PLAYED

The Life of JC Riley

Joel C Riley &
Holly L O'Connor

Copyright © 2018 by Holly O'Connor

All rights reserved. No part of this publication may be reproduced, distributed, or transmitted in any form or by any means, including photocopying, recording, or other electronic or mechanical methods, without the prior written permission of the publisher, except in the case of brief quotations embodied in critical reviews and certain other noncommercial uses permitted by copyright law. For permission requests, write to the publisher at hoc@hoconsulting.com

The Cards I Was Dealt The Hand That I Played

*****

Dedicated to

Paul O'Connor

and

Justin, Janae and Justice

and

The United States Marine Corp

and

Everyone who came from nothing and

continues to fight

and

All the people who believed in me when I didn't

believe in myself

Introduction

Joel and I wrote this book together. This book is all factual to the best of our memories. We want readers to understand the severe disadvantages that some children have growing up. We want to give hope and advice to those in similarly difficult situations. Growing up in an environment without a loving, nurturing and caring family causes great trauma, prevents learning and causes great difficulties for these children later in life. Joel was taken away from his drug addicted mother at the age of two. From age two to twelve he lived in four foster homes. He came to live with Paul and me when he was 12. He was a psychological mess and terribly difficult to deal with. Joel could not believe someone would take him in, love him and really care about him. He did not trust anybody and would not let anyone into his world to help him. He put up a *wall* and refused to listen to us. The only reason we all stuck together so long was because of the amazing strength and values of my husband Paul. Paul has deep religious convictions and a never give up attitude.

All of us grew tremendously through the experience of living together and becoming a real family. We learned how to love, care, understand and forgive each other under some of the most difficult circumstances. We wanted share some of our experiences with you.

Chapter One

The farthest back I can remember is age two. At that time, I was being taken away from my mom, Janice Lott. I did not really understand what or why this was happening. I was going into foster care. A large man came to take my brother, Daniel, and I away. Daniel was two years older than I was. I never thought of him as a half-brother because we grew up together, but he had a different father.

Later I learned that Janice had seven children. The oldest one was Avery. He had Janice's maiden name, Pipes, as his last name. Then there was Carlton and Daniel who both had Lott as their last name. I came next, Joel C. Riley. My birth father was

Chris Riley. I was told that, after I was born, my mother was in a car accident and got a large cash settlement. She got deep into gambling and started doing crack cocaine. This is around the time that we were taken from her. She later had three more children, Shara, Jose, and Ezel. They had a different father. I was the only son of Chris Riley.

We were taken to a Miss O'Neil's house. Miss O'Neil was a Caucasian woman who lived on the south side of Chicago. Daniel and I were left on our own running around the streets until dark, totally unsupervised. Children this age need to be supervised and disciplined. We were just on our own.

When I was three or so, Miss O'Neil took us to Disney World to see James Brown. One of her relatives knew James Brown. All I really remember is riding on the Monorail. The view from the Monorail train was fascinating because I got to see all these things passing by out the window below me and in the distance. I did not realize where I was, at Disney World, because I was too young to know. After a year or two, we were taken away from Miss O'Neil's (I later learned that she was found to be negligent by the Illinois Department of Children and Family Services, DCFS, because she let us run around in the streets, totally unsupervised).

My next bad set of cards I was dealt was being sent to live with another foster lady, Miss Brown on 114th and Vincennes, on the south side of Chicago. Miss Brown was an African American woman. My life took a drastic turn the worst living with Miss Brown. That was about the time I decided that I was going to be street smart rather than book smart, because I felt that I needed the street smarts to survive and thought I would live only a year or two.

So, right now we are transferring homes to Miss Brown's house. She lives in a house in the Morgan Park area. Everything seemed cool at first. She appeared to be a nice outgoing church lady. She was a registered nurse at Southtown Medical Center and took us to Church. I was five and Daniel was seven. But soon after we came to realize that she only had foster children to get a monthly check. The behavior she exhibited when we first met was all a front to get money.

She started abusing us, from the beginning. Whenever Daniel and I were playing around or got into some mischief, we were hit with electric cords, belts or whatever happened to be convenient for Miss Brown. I had a big mouth as far back as I can remember. I got hit more often than Daniel because I was always sassing back to Miss Brown. I started wearing two layers of clothing to protect against the blows. As the years went by, I would ask her if she was done yet or did you get it out of your system, just to piss her off.

Miss Brown had a nice garden out back. She had us working there, weeding and tending to the fruits and vegetables. Every year she would make wine from her grapes. She would put the grapes in a container for me to stomp on. I was the only one who had small enough feet to fit in the container. I tried to drink the wine after it was made without Miss Brown knowing it. The wine made me sick. I do not like wine to this day.

Catholic Charities used to run foster care programs in Chicago and elsewhere in Illinois for the Department of Children and Family Services. I was taken care of through Catholic Charities. The Catholic Charity programs were well run. They had extra-activities for us and they really cared about the children. Catholic Charities gave up doing foster care in Cook County because they could not get insurance after they had to settle a lawsuit involving the mistreatment of three children by a foster parent. It is a shame because it was a great organization. Miss Brown received a stipend every month from Catholic Charities.

Miss Brown never spent the money she received from Catholic Charities on us. I knew some of the money was supposed to be spent on us, but at the time, I was too young to say anything to anyone. She started buying Cadillacs and taking trips. Another girl named Janice who was about the same age as Daniel, lived with us. At first, I thought she was Miss Brown's daughter. Later I learned that Janice was the daughter of some big-time drug dealer that Miss Brown had an arrangement with. Janice was put in charge of Daniel and me, when Miss Brown was away during the day or overnight. Janice was the only one with a key to the house. So, if she did not let us in we were out of luck and had to find other sleeping arrangements.

Daniel and I got each other up to go to grammar school. Two years passed by and I saw parents visiting the school, dropping off and picking up their children at school in their cars or walking their children to and from school. Miss Brown never showed up at school and never treated us like we were her children. I could see that we did not live like a typical family. I decided that I am never going to have a family, so I pretended I did not want one. I didn't want to prepare myself for something that sadly I knew was never going to happen. I decided at that time I was going to control my own life. As a seven-year-old I thought I was gifted and cursed at the same time. I thought being able to survive by myself was a gift and I was good at it. Somehow, I knew I was cursed because I thought I needed to do things that were bad, just to survive.

Every Saturday Miss Brown would kick us out of the house and then, lock the door. We were not given food or sandwiches. We had to stay outside and were not allowed to return. Daniel and I made some friends. Sometimes parents of our friends looked after us and fed us. Then one day I met an older guy. He started giving me lunch money and advice. He knew about my living situation. He was the guy that I looked up to the most and he was a Gangster Disciple, better known in Chicago as GDs. I fell in love with the Gangster Disciples because they were cool and always had money that they shared. I did not sell drugs for them. I knew I was a leader and not a follower because I refused to follow anybody but myself.

This is about the time I started stealing from teachers and stuff like that to survive because Miss Brown did not feed us or take care of us. My brother, Daniel, was older and bigger than I was, and he protected me. He was always hungry. I stole so Daniel could eat. He never made me do it. I just felt that it was my job. I was happy with candy, a glazed donut, or a moon pie, and that was cool back then. The arrangement worked for me. I was never taught to eat properly. Nutritious food was not something that I needed to survive. Nobody cared, and it did not really bother me at the time. I didn't realize how bad a diet of sugar and potato chips was for a growing mind and body. I just ate what I wanted to eat. I also grew a thick skin to be able to tolerate the surroundings. Over the years my skin got thicker and thicker. I knew what I could bear and could not bear.

With time, I had really developed the sense of control by stealing and got pretty good at it. When I say I developed a sense of control, I didn't necessarily want to do it, but I needed to do it. I decided that I was happier when I was in control even if it was not the right thing to do. I understand what it like to be hungry and not cared for. I was not stealing just to steal. I thought I need to do it to survive. I started stealing money from the teachers, often as much as $300 or $400. I did not know what money was except I needed it to buy food, because I was young and dumb. One day, Miss Brown found a book bag full of the money. She asked me where I got it. I said, "I saved it". It was all $1 bills. I thought it could be true. Miss Brown did not like my answer.

In those days they had railings on the stairs going to the basement. Those thick hard handrails rails had short supports screwed into the drywall. The railing reminded me of a pool stick only thicker.

She just grabbed the railing and ripped it right out of the wall and cracked me on the head with it. At the time, I was thinking to myself, I am, like, okay, because I was used to getting beaten by her. Then things got blurry for a minute. The next thing I remember was waking up outside on the lawn. Miss Brown had some vice grips stuck to my ear and she was squeezing them. I passed out, again. My brother, Daniel, at the time was more upset with the way that it happened than I was. He generally kept all his emotions inside and I just dealt with it. I told him, "Do not worry about it, one day we are not going to be in this situation".

Being a foster child through Catholic Charities and in foster care, I knew that there were many people that were trying to help you. I like would like to thank Catholic Charities. Without them, I would not be who I am today. Years later, when I went back to visit the office, I met many folks who remembered me from there and asked about me. They really seemed to care about who I was, and some knew my potential. I thought I was growing up in a fairy tale, though often not the good kind. You never know how you are going to get treated. Based on my experience most foster parents do not care about the children. They just take in children for the money. You never know if a foster family is going to want you or to keep you. So, at that age I decided not to have the feelings, either for love or anything else.

It goes back to being taken from my mother at age two. Now, as I have gotten older in life, I really hated and resented my mother, not because she was my mother but because of the fact that I never learned what real love was. Recently, someone told me the reason I was so hyper is because I never had someone to tell me to calm down and I kind of understood that for a moment. I never respected my mother. I consider how badly I treated women later in my life. I gave them no respect. I had no sense of morals or etiquette. I felt that my mother did not love me, so why should any other woman love me. That is the way I looked at it. I made myself just go against all women. Love is the only thing a kid wants when he is young, and I did not have it.

Back to the time with Miss Brown. As the years progressed I was still in school and I had my good days and my bad days. I will mention one story which I regret, and it is a shame that it became a part of me. One time, we were kicked out the house for a whole week. We slept outside or on the floor of some friend's house. One day I decide to go to church down the street, right on the corner of 111th and Vincennes. I sort of knew what I was about to do was bad, but I had not really learned any better at the time. I figured that the Church gets a lot of money from tithing. I thought since the parishioners had enough money to tithe, I thought that surely, they had enough to give to some poor kid just trying to survive. I knew some of the people in the congregation. So, I went to the Church and I waited for the people to leave their seats to go another area of the church. Then, I went through all the women purses that I could, to find money. When I found the money, I put it in my pocket. I did not think at the time – I am in a church; how could I be doing this? It did not seem bad to me to take some money because it was me trying to survive, in the only way I knew how to survive, which was stealing. It did make me feel awkward, but I knew I was doing it for a good reason. This was a hard habit to get rid of for many years, because it made me feel like I had control of the situation when I could take something from another person. But still, there was me stealing and getting into all this mischief and it affected the way I acted for years to come.

As the years go on, Miss Brown continues to neglect us and abuse us. We knew we were not like normal children. We had to sleep in the basement. I had to take a bath in a cast iron sink that was split in two and was used for laundry during the day. It was terrible at the time and I was always acting out.

Catholic Charities tried to put me in therapy. I was convinced that therapy was never going to work for me. I had the attitude that the therapists and counselors were trying to get into my personal business, so I just shut them out. I did not want anyone knowing anything about me. I would start out with a new therapist and only let him or her get so far and then I would put up the *wall*. I still do this today. The *wall* was and is the cover for my true feelings. I was not going to show my cards to anyone. I still never really let anyone see the real me. With all the therapists I had, I got a kick out of watching them try to figure me out. I was always trying to figure out them, and what I could do to see their cards and to push their buttons. They always tried to get me to talk, to figure out what was going in my head. The *wall* was there for them to go around, but they did not really pay attention. I would pretty much sit on the couches and I would look at them like I was crazy. They would ask me something about my mom, who I never really knew and pry into my other parts of my life. I started to learn and think that I could control the mind of another person. I felt that doing so put me one up on them. They were playing mind games with me, so I was going to play mind games with them. I understood that at an early age.

I never wanted to be dependent on anyone. I valued the mind games and thought that they put me in control and made me strong. I knew that therapy was supposed to help me. But I was not going to let it help me. I had a strong sense that all the questions they were asking were my own personal business. My personal business was not for outsiders to know. My personal business was not something I wanted the therapists or caseworkers to put into their files or become a case study for discussion with other people, like I am crazy.

When I was seven years old, I first learned about sex. A fifteen-year-old girl name Lashonda started abusing me. I thought we were just playing house and did not really know what that meant. She would unbutton my pants and play with my private parts. They only thing, I knew about sex was you stick something in something else. We had sex and at the time I did not associate it with feelings or love. I just thought that fuck just meant to fuck. I was only 7 years old you and I did not know who to tell. I did not believe that anyone would believe me if I did. I did not look at it like I was abused or raped. I just thought I was the man. Meaning when I say "man", I was just doing what I saw on television and watched people doing openly in the neighborhood. In my mind, I thought I was getting all the praise because I am 7 years old and I am having sex with a 15-year-old. I did not know until later that this really messed up my brain.

Worse yet, for years to come, I thought sex was just something just to do, instead of something of that had to do with passion or feeling. I never associated it with me falling in love with somebody or having an intimate relationship with a person. I just thought of it as a thrill and just did it because it was there to do. Later in my life, I had to understand why things happened the way they did. When you are young and have no supervision, you are pretty much doing what you want to do and take part in what is going on around you. We imitated things on television. Playing house every Saturday with different girls did not mean just to pretend to be cooking and cleaning or pretending to be a family. Back then I did not know what a family was. This created a mental block for me that messed me up later in my life.

Miss Brown always had a .38 gun under her mattress and she had another .45 in the closet. Of course, we knew where they were and what they were. We lived in an area that was still predominantly African-American with gangs and drugs. It was not that bad, but most people had guns. Tyrone was my best friend at the time. He was bad just like me. His brother had rank in the gang meaning he had power. They looked out for me and became my second family.

The first school that I attended was a Catholic School, Holy Name of Mary. I got kicked out of first grade. I was in class one day and a girl stabbed me in my head with a pencil. I started bleeding. Blood always freaked me out and stirred up anger inside of me, ever since the day at Miss Brown's house when I saw a rat walk into a trap that crushed him and spewed some blood all around the trap. I exploded with anger after being stabbed. I took the pencil from the girl and stabbed her in the face with it. I did not care if I was hurting her. I did not even think about it. Then I took a ruler and started smacking her with it. The teacher, a nun, tried to take the ruler from me. I grabbed it back and started hitting the nun with it. At that time, I had an anger management problem, because I always held everything inside. When someone treated me badly or pissed me off, I just blew up. I did not know how to deal with it any other way. I could not express myself well and teachers and others seemed to blame me, even if I did not start something. Later, I learned that that happens to a child when he/she bottles up all the feelings. The anger eventually comes out and you are not able to control it.

Needless to say, I got expelled from the Holy Name of Mary. I was transferred to Esmond. Esmond was a public school, so you do not have to wear uniforms. I was happy about that. At this time, I am still with Daniel at Miss Brown's. It is still the early 90s and I am learning about myself. I thought most kids in foster care get physically abused because that was my experience.

Miss Brown had a family member who also abused us. He was an older man that told me to take off my clothes and I wondered why. He did not touch my private parts. He just looked at me and I was like okay, this is weird. As a child you do not know anything else. He touched my back and it was a shock to my nerves. I told my brother what happened to me. Daniel said he wanted to kill this person. Then he disappeared for about a week. He left me all alone at Miss Brown's.

Later I learned that Danny was trying to get help for us by letting DCFS know that we were being abused. I was seriously worried about him. I just hung on. I felt like I had to hang on to survive. I thought about what I would do to survive without Daniel. I had pretty much accumulated so much money from the streets by stealing that I thought I really had enough money just to go on my own.

In a couple of days, I was taken from Miss Brown by the police. I was thinking, is this really happening and are they going to split up Daniel and me? I was happy that I was leaving Miss Brown's. I did not know whether I would see my brother again or where I was going. I just knew I had to be mentally tough especially no longer having my brother around.

Catholic Charities then sent just me to a family in Flossmoor Hills, Illinois. They had decided to split up Daniel and me. The new family was the Wheelers, Tina and Harry Wheeler. They already had five foster children who all came from the same family. It was awkward because as soon as I got there I seemed to know that, they were going to end up adopting all them except for me. I knew at that point I was not going part of their family. But, I still wanted to be part of a family. I was there for a year or two. The family was nice. I was going to Parker Junior High. I was bad at learning how to read. I was always hyperactive and angry that I could not perform well in class. I always thought I could perform if I wanted to. I always said that I did not do well because I did not want to. I figured it was more fun being the class clown than behaving in class. I now realize that when you are a child and as angry and hyperactive as I was at that age, it is not really a matter of choice. I was not physically able to concentrate.

The Wheelers lived in a nice quiet suburban neighborhood. They were a beautiful African-American family. I just assumed that they would not want me at the end of the day. I knew I was going to end up leaving, probably because I thought it was too nice and nothing nice ever lasted in my case. At seven and eight years old, I was already putting up the *wall*. I already had a mental block and started to make things fail intentionally because I did not think I was worth anything good happening to me.

I thought would probably stay at the Wheelers for two years or so. I knew I was going to be sent to another home when I got a new pair of gym shoes or new clothes. This happened to me and other foster kids from Catholic Charities. Then one day or two after getting a new outfit my caseworker came to get me and told me I was moving again, back into the city of Chicago. They did not tell me why I was moving. All the Wheelers other foster children stayed with the family. I knew how that hand was going to be played.

I then went to live on 114th and Michigan, the Roseland area. It was called the wild hundreds. I thought at the time that this was my playground. I had the best time of my life. My new foster mom,

Miss Mason seemed to care for me. Miss Mason was not like Miss Brown or Miss O'Neil. I really liked her family. The family members were nice and loving. But, I was still in foster care and I knew this would never last forever. I went to school and did the normal things a child did. I thought I was in a cool situation at the time.

However, I was back in the city of Chicago in the wild hundreds area of the town. It was a wild area. You did not go in the area unless you were a Gangster Disciple. In the area you had Carver high school. Near Carver, you had the Finger and Julie, candy stores. Near 114th and Michigan all the way down I was in sweet stuff heaven. There were all kinds of candy and donut stores. It was home of The Old Fashion Donuts. Candy and other junk food were my substitute for food and a lot of other things.

I never really thought about hating Miss Brown and Miss O'Neil. I never knew how to feel about any of my foster moms. I knew that none of them was my real my mother. I knew that any one of them could be replaced at any time. I still always felt angry inside. At Miss Mason's I was often out on the street and thought I knew about street life until I saw someone get shot.

To this day, I will never forget the time when I got sent to the store to pick up some chicken and rice. I was living in an urban community on the south side, where everyone knows, the Chinese restaurants make good fried chicken and good rice. So, I am in the store picking up the food to bring home to Miss Mason's. There is a bullet proof glass wall between the workers at the restaurant and the customers, because the area has a lot of crime. A couple of older guys came in at the same time. I knew they were GD gang members. They said to me "Hey shorty, ya might want to step back some". They had some words with another customer, who was apparently from a different gang. Then, one of them pulled out a gun and blew the dude's head off. There was blood and brains all over the place. I was so shocked and startled I just stood there frozen. I could not move. I kept looking and started crying and kept looking. Still crying, I touched the blood. The place was a mess and I just kept looking.

At the time, I did not really think that I was a witness to a murder. I was scared because a man was just shot, and I did not know what to do. The fact that I just froze and was not able to do anything about it really touched a nerve. I now know that my reaction was a normal reaction for someone my age, but I was haunted by it for years to come. At the time, I was thinking to myself that now, I am going to get used to seeing people die. I knew I was going to see more murders because of the environment that I lived in. Of course, it happened just like that. I mean, I held my first gun when I was seven years old. I assumed if you live in a foster home or any other home in my neighborhood, that guns were available. It was normal for people to have them and they were kind of like toys of me. I never shot one, but I did have access to guns all my life. I thought I was tough and I did not really need it for protection. I never got into it with anyone. I was always talking to people and most people liked me. I was always articulate and good at busting jokes.

After you see someone die at that young age, your brain does not register the same anymore. I did not understand it at the time and I never knew how it would affect me to this day. Throughout all these years from 2 years old all the way to 12 years old, there were many traumatic events in my life, being taken away from my mother, being abused, and neglected, switching foster homes, etc. I am still working out all the traumatic things that happened in my childhood. I am realizing that most of my life, I lived with traumatic stress.

Because of the stress, I continually shut myself down. I was not trying to hear what people were trying to say to me. I was not trying to be anyone's friend and I was not trying to listen to anyone. I was just trying to survive. I never realized I had post-traumatic stress disorder (PTSD) and that made me different. I felt like I was normal because I thought I did everything else the same as other people do. I was hurting inside, and I never want to be around people. I did not trust anyone.

Here is the autobiography I wrote as a child:

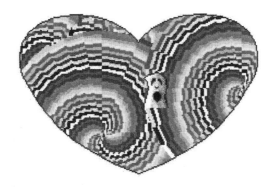

MY AUTOBIGRAPHY

by

JOEL RILEY

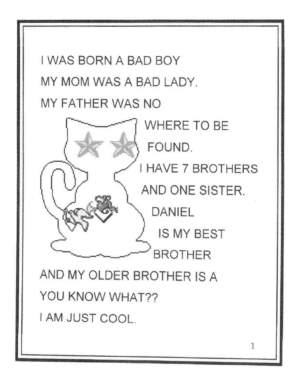

I WAS BORN A BAD BOY
MY MOM WAS A BAD LADY.
MY FATHER WAS NO
WHERE TO BE
FOUND.
I HAVE 7 BROTHERS
AND ONE SISTER.
DANIEL
IS MY BEST
BROTHER
AND MY OLDER BROTHER IS A
YOU KNOW WHAT??
I AM JUST COOL.

1

Joel C Riley – Holly L O'Connor

30

SO I BEEN IN A
LOT OF
FOSTER
HOMES.
THEY WERE ALL BAD. THAT
MAD ME MAD-
VERY MAD!!! I
WAS COOL.
THEN I WAS A
KID. I CAN DANCE AND I CAN
BASKETBALL AND BASEBALL. I

3

CAN TALK ABOUT PEOPLE AND I
COULD BE THE NEXT MAYOR.
I LOOK UP TO GOD AND MY
BROTHER,
AND PENNY. ONE
OF MY GOALS IS TO
STAY IN SCHOOL.

THE END

BY JOEL RILEY

TR

4

I was always angry. I occasionally let people touch me and get a little close. Then when they got too close, I would put up the *wall*. When you store too much behind the *wall*, the *wall* starts to crack, or it blows up. From a young age, I asked God why he lets me remember the things I remember. Unfortunately, my memory it good and hopefully putting the details down on paper may help some others and let you understand why some people are the way they are.

Daniel and I were on TV one Christmas on a segment called a Family for Me. Daniel did not say much. I was leaning in and doing all the talking. The host of the show told me that I was very articulate and said, "maybe you should go into drama or theatre". I thought that the guy was crazy. I find out later this is one of those talents that I have that it helped me later in life. It is just different when you grow up in the urban environment, you adapt to your situation your surroundings. I thought I always have adapted but mentally, I was broken down. I was never really like normal, whatever that is. I knew that and it I never counted against me. I just looked at it like this is what God has in store for me. But I did not see why God could make someone suffer the way he made me. So, I ended up not really believing in him.

I also was thinking at the time "Where is my real father"? A kid is supposed to have a father. When I was a child I remember being with him at a McDonald's. I remember a man with a Jerry curl in his hair. It had to be around 1983-84 and I was with my brother Daniel. I thought at the time that he was my brother Daniel's father. That was the only time I saw him as a child.

Chapter 2

After living in Roseland and seeing the murder, Catholic Charities took me out of Miss Mason's home. She was a nice woman, but she could not deal with all the calls from the school and did not know how to handle me. My case worker brought me to Paul and Holly O'Connor's house for the weekend. This was a whole different world to me.

Their house was in the Lincoln Park, an upper-class area of Chicago, just north of downtown. It was a two-story brick house with limestone trim. They showed me my room. A small clean room with a full-sized bed. I was all geeked out because I saw it was only for me and nobody would be bothering me, though I tried not to show it. I was on my best behavior.

That week they brought me with them to visit some friends who had a beautiful house on a lake in Wisconsin. I slept some in the car. I told them I was tired because I was up late last night studying chemistry. It sounded like something they would have liked to hear me say. I just made it up. I did know all the capitals of all the states in the United States, so I tried to impress them with that. I must have fooled them because they agreed to take me in.

The above paragraph is true. Paul and I coached Little League and tutored in Cabrini Green for a couple of years. Paul thought we could help some children a lot more by having them full time. So, we went to foster parent training.

We had to go through several weekends of training at Catholic Charities before we got our license to be foster parents. They taught us not to put the children in burning hot water or that each child must have their own bed and mattress. We were not allowed to use any physical punishment on the children. I guess DCFS must have had some awful foster parents in the past. If Joel were my birth son, I definitely would have slapped him a few times. I threw a sponge at him once for good measure. He was eating candy before Easter dinner just to annoy me.

When I arrived at the O'Connor's, I was still a shorty. I was cross-eyed, had a squeaky loud voice, and a big chip in my front tooth. I still had the *wall* up. In August, Holly and Paul took me to the eye doctors at Children's Hospital in Lincoln Park and I ended up having surgery to fix my eyes. They also took me to the dentist to get my tooth fixed.

I was amazed that no one took the time to take Joel to the eye doctor to have his eyes looked at. Foster children were all covered by Medicare and an Illinois program called Kids Care so there was no cost. I took him to a clinic in uptown that was part of Children's Memorial Hospital. The doctors and nurses there were great. They would spend more time with Joel and the other children than any private physician spent with me.

The doctor saw Joel and sent him to an eye specialist the next week. The surgeon said the procedure was fairly routine. How could Joel get to be twelve years old and no other caregiver took the time to do anything about his cross eyes? I am sure that having cross eyes was one of the reasons that he had learning difficulties in grade school.

Joel C Riley – Worcester MA 1996

Joel, Paul and Miles Camping

Joel thought he was such a touch guy. When we went for the eye surgery he was such a baby, afraid of needles and going under anesthesia. He wanted gas, but the doctor did not want to give it to him because he was too small. I had to hold his hand the whole time. I sat with him when he got out of surgery and our friend, Margie, came to see him with some gifts. Bringing him home was tough because he was scared and could not see because he was still recovering from the surgery. I think it was pretty traumatic for him. A couple of days later his eyes were perfect.

Holly and Paul were Caucasian – I never really liked that word. They were white, and I was okay with that. They became my mom and dad. However, even though I was there for many years, I still never really trusted them. I put up the *wall* and tested them all the time. I never really shared any of my past experiences with them. I still held my cards close to the vest. I believed that they would give me up and send me to another home. I did a lot of things to make sure they would. If I left, there it had to be because I wanted to go and not because they did not want me. I thought I was in control and was continually seeking something. If I saw something I wanted, I would take it if I could.

Paul came from Worchester, Massachusetts. His Dad was a fireman. Paul played football and got accepted to Columbia College in York City. Paul's father died when Paul was in his first year of college. To me, being a fireman was a middle-class black person's job. He had a great mother who worked hard taking care of her four children. Paul had an older brother, Robert, who also became a fireman. Robert seemed a lot like me because he was hyper and was always running around doing odd jobs for people. Paul's sister Beth was the oldest child in the family. She was a nurse who always seemed very laid back. Paul's sister Jane was 7 years younger than he was. Jane moved to Chicago and married a great guy named Jeff. I liked them both a lot. They took care of me at times when Paul and Holly had to go out of town for work or a vacation from me. I was sick one time and they spoiled me and let me stay home from school. I used to try to stay home from school pretending I was sick, but Paul and Holly often did not believe me. I had to have a fever or be throwing up before the let me stay home. I did throw up on my desk one time, and Paul came and brought me home.

Paul attended the University of Chicago MBA program and then went into the real estate industry.

He worked himself up from the bottom to become a successful real estate developer. Holly was at Barnard College which at the time was the sister school to Columbia College in York City when she me Paul. I have seen pictures of Paul in his football uniform with sideburns. He thought he was pretty cool. I pictured Holly as a geeky nerd, but I am not sure about that. Paul was transferred to Chicago by his employer. A couple of years later, when Holly graduated from Columbia Business School she married Paul and moved to Chicago.

They lived in Lincoln Park an upscale area on the north side of the city. The two of them started coaching little league baseball on the corner of Sedgwick and Division St, which is now a Jewel grocery store. The kids in the baseball league all came from gang infested Cabrini Green and housing projects that surrounded the field. A different gang controlled each building, Vicelords, Cobras, Gangster Disciples, etc. Drug dealings and shootings happened regularly those days. The league was one of many leagues started by Holly and Paul's friend from College, Bob Muzikowski. One of the coaches, who spent summer with the league, wrote a book about the league and Bob, which was made into a movie with Keanu Reeves. The movie's stereotyping of inner city kids so upset Bob, he tried to sue the movie company. He was not successful with the lawsuit, but he went ahead and wrote his own book. Bob now runs Hope Academy, a Christian high school on the west side of Chicago. He and his wife Tina have made a major difference in the lives of many people.

Holly and Paul coached baseball for 13 to 15-year-old boys in Cabrini Green out of the goodness of their hearts. All the teams in the league were named after African Tribes. Holly, Paul, and their friend Margie had the Zulu's. They had lots of stories about the kids they coached that were like family to them. Holly liked it because it was so opposite of what she did during the day. She was a successful tax accountant. She up grew up in New Jersey. She was tough, and she enjoyed being around the kids trying to keep them out of trouble in the summer. She also knew more about baseball at the time than did Paul. They would shout back and forth at each other on the field. Holly was usually right.

Paul told me the story about a boy on his baseball team, named Tim. Tim left Chicago when he was 15 to live with his mother and sister in Milwaukie. When Tim was 16 he shot and killed another gang member who was harassing his sister. Tim refused to implicate the other gang members or tell anyone where he got the gun. He was sentenced to life in jail. Most of the other kids they coached over the years never had much of a chance and ended up in gangs and or jail. Paul thought that he could better help the kids if he had them full time rather than just for a few hours a week. That is when they decided to become foster parents. Paul's job was more flexible than Holly's work, so he took over most of the parenting, going to school meetings, etc.

Paul and Holly would take me up to Wisconsin to visit Tim in a maximum-security prison outside of Milwaukee. They thought visiting Tim would help me avoid getting into trouble and ending up like him. Tim was actually a smart and thoughtful person who made a big mistake when he was young. He had anger issues and a temper like me. Tim became somewhat of a big brother to me. I know he is still serving his sentence and may be eligible for parole in the next several years.

Life takes strange turns. Everybody makes mistakes because nobody is perfect. I will never be perfect, and I am fine with that. I understand that God did not make me to be that way. Today, I realize that you can be in control and carry out many things. You first must understand who you are. You have to figure out what want in your life and start to make changes, one step at a time. I thought I could never change who I was. From 2 years old always been the same person, rude, obnoxious, loud, and arrogant. I was self-driven, hyper and could talk shit all day.

Parents had to go through training and background checks before they could become foster parents at Catholic Charities. They also ask them what type of child they preferred, for example will they be comfortable with a person of a particular race, homosexual, an obese or medical needs child. Holly asked for a quiet boy. When I turned up, I had a loud squeaky voice and cross-eyes. I would not eat most foods, not anything healthy anyway. I would absolutely refuse to do any homework or take any tutoring.

Holly thought, at first, I would not last three months. She told me she had to pretend to like me at first and would come and hug me and kiss me every morning and night. I was hard to like or love. Later, she told me that having me as a son taught her that is was possible to learn to truly love someone and really forgive people like she was never able to do before.

Honestly, I never believed in the devil before Joel came to live with us. The first time Paul and I took Joel to Sunday mass, I thought I was watching a version of The Exorcist. Joel had just come to live with us. He was small and shook like crazy and his face went into contortions, like I have never seen before. I could see the devil in him. I prayed for years after that and still do so that the devil would leave him. Paul did not notice. The first summer he was with us, our good friend Margie, who coached the Zulu baseball team with us was between jobs. She had work as a terminal manager for United Airlines. She looked after Joel for a couple of months that summer. She was great with the kids and was enormously intuitive and sensitive. She was also a strong believing Christian. She was the only one I told about the devil being in Joel. For some reason I knew she would not think I was crazy. When I told her, she said, "No doubt about it, I am praying too".

Since Paul grew up from a poor family and put himself through college, I had to listen to many lectures on self-reliance. He mowed lawns and painted and bought a car before he had his driver's license. I thought these were all anachronisms since I did not see these types of people in my lifetime. I call him my guardian angel. He does things that most people would not think of doing and he does them from the bottom of his heart. He always thought that he was not doing enough for others. I could never figure out why did not give up on me. I asked him one day and he told me, "God told him not to". As many times as, I tried to stir the pot up he was still there for me. He is one of the few people I have great respect for. I used to test him all the time. He would ask me what 2 and 2 was and I would not answer or say 7. He also got angry when I wore my hat to the side like a gang member or when I would not tuck in my shirt. I knew how to push his buttons. I like who Paul is, but I know I cannot be like him. I am not him and have to be myself. I understand that.

Holly grew up in New Jersey, on the other side of life, the better side. Her father worked his ass off and her mother is a fabulous artist. Holly also had a brother with a lovely wife. Holly always worked hard because she wanted to be the boss. Not like a boss as in bossing around people. She wanted to be independent and not rely a man or on anyone else. I congratulate her for that. Holly told me, she made mistakes along the way and learned from them. I want my daughter to grow up the same way, strong and self-reliant.

When I first moved in with the O'Connors, I only had about 3 outfits. One was a matching set of yellow and grey plaid shorts and a shirt. They had dirt and stains on them. I loved them because it was one of the few outfits I got to pick them out at Miss Masons. My other things were equally as raggedy. I liked Holly because she would bring me new clothes when she came home from work. She had to walk through Carson Pirie Scot on her way to EL and would pick up things for me on sale. Paul on the other hand, never thought I needed much of anything new. He kept his clothes for years and would tell me so constantly.

Paul and Holly started with nothing and built themselves up. However, the success of the parent has little to do with the success of the child. Your children are going to do what they want to do regardless of what you set out for them. Growing up in Lincoln Park I had a lot of opportunities was exposed to a lot of different things. The other kids would tell me, " hey do you know are growing up around millionaires and you are just a poor black kid". I never wanted to be a millionaire. I did not think it would make me happy. I am a Libra and I always been a giving person. As a matter of fact, I usually stole for other people so that I could give then something. My mother and father were shocked because one of my teachers told them that they should not be giving me so much candy. I always bought my own candy with my allowance or money I took from my Holly's purse and was handing it out to the other kids. Paul and Holly almost never had candy around the house. Holly is a vegetarian and we always had healthy food at home.

When I had a dollar or two, I thought I was rich. I was always thinking of ways to turn money into more money. I would go and buy candy to bring to school and sell it or give it away to make friends. I had always heard about congressmen and other politicians were crooked. I thought if they made money that way I could do it too. I was not good at math. My friend James Otis was very smart and tried to help me with school work. I also learned some math from being around people selling drugs. I learned that 8 ounces is half a pound of marijuana and how much a gram of cocaine was.

I do now believe you should listen to your parents. At first it goes in one ear and out the other, blah, blah blah. I also thought you should learn how to play both of your parents. Now I realize that your parents are trying to make things better for you in the future. Unfortunately, one does not realize this until later in life.

Chapter 3

My new foster parents opened my eyes to a lot of things. We took a car trip to the east coast to pick up one of the baseball players from Cabrini Green, that Paul and Holly had been mentoring. He was at summer school at the Taft boarding school in Connecticut. Holly and Paul talked about what a great kid Miles was and how I would really like him. When we met, Miles and I took an immediate dislike towards each other. Miles was mad because he used to have all of Holly and Paul's attention and here comes me, the new kid, a short kid with a squeaky high, loud voice.

Miles was two years or so older than I was. We picked him up and drove to Cape Cod, Massachusetts to visit Paul's sister Beth and her husband, Jim. Beth is a nurse and Jim was a six-foot five-inch parole officer. I started right in on Miles trying to make him angry. Miles retaliated. We were both ragging on each other. Beth suggested that she and Jim take us for a walk. Jim had to physically separate us when we started dissing each other's mother and we were about to go at each other. Holly and Paul were upset but glad that Jim and Beth were there to stop us.

Miles was Holly and Paul's" Godson". He was on their baseball team, the Zulus. Holly and Paul got him into Provident St Mel, an all-black college preparatory high school on Chicago's West Side through a non-profit called Highsight. This non-profit was started by one of the baseball coaches to get inner city kids from Cabrini Green into private high school and prepare them for college. Highsight has been successful and has helped numerous inner-city kids get into and stay in college. Miles used to stay over the O'Connor's house one or two nights a week, so Paul could tutor him. He decided to move in with the O'Connor's too, when he saw that I was moving in. Miles lived with his single mom and sister on the West Side of Chicago in a one-bedroom apartment. His mom was okay with it because she agreed with the O'Connors about discipline and school. I thought Miles was going to be the good son and I would be the bad son. They had to wear uniforms at St. Mel. I was not into uniforms and school. I wanted to wear Michael Jordan sneakers (even though I did not have any) and I could not wear them at a private school. I failed the St. Mel entrance exam on purpose. I did not even try, probably because I was afraid of not passing. I was still thinking I was not going to stay long at the O'Connor's.

I went to the first half of 7th grade at the Lincoln Elementary school which was a few blocks from the O'Connors. I was still acting up but doing okay. The entire school was in the band. I played the drums.

Joel did not do badly at Lincoln Elementary school. He had some good teachers and was in some special education classes. One day, the principle from the school called to tell us that Joel had gotten into a fight. When we went to pick him up, it turned out that one of the teachers watched the whole thing. Paul had told Joel that he was not allowed to hit anyone unless he was hit three times first. According to the teacher, a larger boy was picking on Joel and hit him three times. Joel waited for the third blow and then he wailed on the bully.

Everyone concluded Joel acted in self-defense and was not disciplined.

Around this time Catholic Charities took Joel to see his birth Mom who he did not remember. She was homeless and never took care of any of her children. Joel did not want to go and see her. Catholic Charities thought he should go and Joel was technically under their care. Whenever, he went to visit her, he would come home, and we would ask him how it went. He would put up the wall and say "fine, no big deal". Then two or three days later he would explode in school and get suspended. It was like clockwork. Later reading about foster children and other abused children, I learned that this is common. They try to hold everything in, but then they explode.

I don't remember much about seeing my mother. Catholic Charities took me down to see my mother a couple of times. I did not want to go and did not feel anything for her. I soon started not listening to Holly or Paul and would not do any homework. I would not eat anything when I was around them. One day I was playing around the house with some friends and broke the glass in the front door. I called the police to tell them a burglar tried to break in. Paul came home to find a Policeman standing in the front of the house. The policeman was great. He knew we kids had broken the door because the glass was on the outside of the house not the inside. I kept lying and saying that I did not do it.

> *Joel was not really a good liar. When he was sitting down his knees would start shaking. It was a dead giveaway. He would also tell us stories about what bad thing "some other boy" did in class. It usually turned out to be Joel instead of the "other boy".*

I kept testing and testing them. Paul, Holly, Miles, and I went to family counselling at Catholic Charities. I would clam and act tough for the whole sessions. One day, I lied about leaving the front door open by mistake. I was told many times to make sure it was locked. The O'Connors did not think it was a terrible thing that I left the door open, but they hated when I lied to them. I would not say I was wrong and that I lied. Paul and I got into it. The family ended up going to a meeting at Catholic Charities. It was right around Christmas time. They all decided to send me to Maryville Academy, a campus of group homes in Des Plaines, Illinois for abandoned and troubled children that was run by Catholic Charities. I thought I was in control.

Maryville was actually a nice place. I liked being there. I lived in a group home which was shared with nine to twelve other homeless children. They had a point system at Maryville. You got positive and negative points every day. Doing chores, making your bed, and cleaning up were positive points. Bad attitude, talking back, doing badly in school were negative points. Everyone was supposed to be net positive at the end of the day and the week. I knew how to play the game with the various people in charge of the house and what I needed to do to keep my points positive. Sometimes, I could not help being negative. I knew the consequences.

Fortunately, I was able to come home to the O'Connors' on the weekends and see my friends. Paul often came up during the week to watch me play my basketball games.

Joel was good on the weekends. Catholic Charities brought him home in a van every Friday brought him back on Sunday nights. Paul had him under control and took him to play sports, hockey and basketball and they would go to the movies, to see "guy movies".

Joel really like to play with people's minds. He was also good at reading the type of people he met. We had a woman friend over one day and Joel said something like she is thinks she has it all going for her. He was right. I would watch Joel trying to test Paul and set Paul off. I would tell Paul that Joel was playing him, and Paul would still get angry. I had to retreat to my bedroom to avoid the commotion. I am not a confrontational person unless I have to be.

Joel and Miles would start fighting when I got home from work. I would ignore them and start to go upstairs to get away. They would follow me up the stairs arguing and punching each other. I knew they were just looking for attention. They were not going to get my attention by fighting with each other. It got old after a while.

I really thought at the time, that I was working the system. I thought I was in control and never let anyone get the upper hand. I still had the wall up and never showed anyone my hand or feelings. I was controlling the deck. I did not care if someone was smarter or even trying to be helpful. I just knew I was articulate and could make people mad. I would never back down from a challenge. I was disciplined a lot and was often denied a pass to go home on the weekend from Maryville. It really did not bother me because it meant that I could stay and play basketball.

I was good at basketball then. I had great moves and great speed. I just wanted to dribble and show off with my Michael Jordan shoes on my feet. Michael Jordan shoes were all the rage in the black community. Every time a new model came out I wanted it. They were twice the price of ordinary basketball shoes. The O'Connor's would only pay for the price of regular basketball shoes. I had to earn the other half doing extra chores and projects around the house.

Maryville was not a bad place. They tried to take us to various places. I often did not go when they went to the movies because that is what I did with Paul when I went home on the weekends. Holly usually did not come, because she did not like the choice of movies, almost always guy flicks about sports or violence. The O'Connor's would send me back to Maryville with some food for the week, some semi-nutritious stuff like cereal, fruit gushers and Gogurt sticks. I did not like the food at Maryville.

I did well enough at Maryville to be allowed to come back to O'Connor's house for 9th grade. I was going to Lincoln Park High School. I came to school with a big chip on my shoulder. I was around 5 feet 3, 5 feet 4, a little guy. But I am thinking that I am threat now, all cool in my Jordan's. The first day of school my schedule was not ready, so I did not have to go to class. I end up wandering around the school checking out the upper classmen and sizing everybody up.

These were the days of Cabrini Green, the big project where Holly and Paul coached baseball. Many of the kids from Cabrini came to Lincoln Park High. The kids from Cabrini were GD's and Stones gang members. I tried to stay under the radar because I never clicked with them. When I was sixteen, I met my future wife, Courtney. She lived just around the corner from my house. We were friends at first. She lived with her step-mother, Diane, who was white, and her father was Puerto Rican. Her birthmother was black and lived further up north. Courtney was cute and had a lot of energy. I told Courtney that she would be my wife the first time I met her.

One day, Joel came home from high school without his keys. This was at least the third or fourth time in several months he had lost his keys. Paul started getting on Joel's case. Joel said, he did not lose them and that he knew where there were. Joel said they were in a garbage can at school. Paul did not believe him and took Joel up to the school yard. It was cold and rainy. Paul made Joel stand there and take out all the stuff in the large metal can to see if Joel was telling the truth.

In the can were hundreds of sandwiches and lunches that the students just threw away. All the nicely packed sandwiches parents made for their kids. It turned out that Joel's key was at the bottom of the can. Joel was mouthing off to one of the big guys at school, and the guy picked up Joel and turned him upside down into the can. Paul had to apologize for not believing Joel.

Paul was also the one that made the Joel and Miles sandwiches in the morning. Joel said to Paul that he liked the sandwiches so much, and could Paul make him two every day. Paul was happy because he thought Joel was eating something reasonably healthy for Joel. We later found out that Joel would eat one, unlike the other kids who were throwing them away, and sell the other one to a buddy.

During my freshman orientation I met this girl named Jonnetta. She had a crush on me. She was asking everyone that knew me who is this guy. Everyone told her to stay away from me. I already had a bad reputation. I thought I was like okay and just a normal person. I later met her, and she was a cool person. We ended up dating. I made the football team and I could have made the track team, but I did not want to run. I made the basketball team but shortly thereafter the coach tossed me off because of my badass mouth. We did not see eye to eye.

Joel did play football even though he was on the small side. He was short, but he was tough and usually quite fast. We were at his first game. Joel catches a ball and another kid three times his size clocks him. We thought Joel was knocked out. The coach brought him to the sidelines to rest. Joel came to the sideline and started screaming for the team.

I decided to apply myself and had a decent GPA my freshman year because I did not want to go to summer school. However, I was still fighting the system. Every time I started to do well, something inside me said I was not worth it. I would then start to sabotage myself. I now wish I had fought harder for myself and realized what was important at that time. I start acting out in class and keep getting in trouble. The kids came to school with gin in their apple juice. I started drinking with them and showing off. But, I made it through freshman year and did not have to go summer school.

Paul used to drop Miles and Joel off at school every day. He dropped Joel off at Lincoln Park High and then drove Miles to Provident St. Mel on the west side. St Mel was a great school. The emphasis was integrity and hard work.

One day, Miles and Joel were arguing in the car, not uncommon at all, on the way to Lincoln Park High. Joel climbed out of the car but stepped back in toward the car to punch Miles. Paul thought Joel was out of the car and rolled forward on to Joel's foot. Joel started screaming. Paul immediately stopped the car and looked out the window. The rear wheel of the car was on Joel's foot. Paul rolled off Joel's foot and drove away, yelling back at Joel that he better go to school. Joel continued on to school.

The school called me mid-morning and told me to come and get Joel. They said he could not walk on his foot. I picked him up at school and we went to Children's Hospital. At that time, the hospital was just around the block from the school. I remember it because Joel would not tell the doctor how he hurt his foot. Whenever a foster child is taken to the hospital with an injury, the hospital is required to report it to Catholic Charities or DCFS. Joel was afraid that he would be taken away from us or that Paul would get into trouble.

I did tell the doctor what happened. Joel got his foot wrapped. There was a minor crack in one of the bones of Joel's foot. Joel went to school with crutches the next day. When he found out that he had a football game the coming Saturday, he's foot miraculously healed in two days.

The O'Connors sent Miles and me to New York military academy for two weeks in the summer. Miles was taking SAT prep and I was taking a couple of short courses. Donald Trump went there for high school. I also went to basketball camp to get away from Chicago and have new experiences.

I do now believe you should listen to your parents. At first it goes in one ear and out the other, blah, blah blah. I also thought you should learn how to play both of your parents. Now I realize that your parents are trying to make things better for you in the future. Unfortunately, one generally doesn't realize this until later in life.

Chapter 4

Currently, I am just going into my sophomore year at Lincoln Park High School. I had just had the best year of my life. I transitioned from Maryville Academy back to the O'Connor's and went through a year of Lincoln Park High with decent grades. I had friends and the girls were crushing on me. I got to play a lot of basketball at New York Military Academy and I thought I was good. I did some studying in class there. But at Lincoln Park High, I started just kicking it. From here on I will start referring to the O'Connors to as my parents, because they stuck with me through these years. Paul especially because he could never give up on me. Holly was always working, business, business, business and would not put up with my bullshit.

But, by the time the Fall came, I had my head stuck up my ass. I think "I'm the man" in my head and I think I can do whatever the fuck I want to do. I start making bad bets and playing the wrong cards. Once I started doing well, I always managed to screw things up. Self-sabotage, I could not help it.

I am still at Lincoln Park High School. We now had classes and with the upper classmen. Freshmen were separated from the other grades. I thought I would just hang out and do whatever I could to be noticed. What I thought was cool was from the ghetto, wearing Jordon's and jewelry and having a gang of friends around. Fuck class, fuck the teachers. I did not care about anything important. My parents hired a strong Russian woman, Zita, to look after the house from three onward, the time I was supposed to be home from school. She took charge, until my parents got home from work. I knew she would be there at three so, I started bringing friends to the house after third period.

One day at school, there was a group of us hanging around campus and there was some kind of skirmish going on. I was not involved. The police tried to disperse the crowd and told us to go home. Most of the black kids went south to Cabrini Green. I headed east towards home. I could have just gone around the block, but I decided to argue with the police officers. One of the police officers shouted at me "black kids don't live over that way". I proceeded to argue with the officers, and they put me in the paddy wagon and took me to the police station. Paul had to pick me up at the police station. The police never apologized.

My house was three blocks away from Lincoln Park High School. I became popular. I wanted to be with the in-crowd even though I knew I was better than they were. My friends and I got into the liquor cabinet at home. Every day was a party. It did not last too long because Zita, the housekeeper, would show up early. I would make up some bullshit about being let out early from school that day. Nobody really believed me. We were drinking way too early in life.

I also started learning to shoot dice. I thought it was a great way to make money. My now brother Miles got caught shooting dice in the bathroom at Provident St Mel. He was trying to get fifty cents more for the bus ride home from school or at least that is what he told our parents. The janitor caught the two guys in the boy's room and they were sentenced to three Saturdays at the school, cleaning with the janitor. When I played dice, I figured out how to play so I usually won. I was swindling money from friends and others who were not too bright. My mom started finding dice around the house and would throw them away, but I always got more. We got the usual lectures from our parents on the evils of gambling. Both Miles and I did not pay attention. If we had, it would have saved us both some trouble later in life.

I continued to act out in school and often got detention with Mr. Jordon, the vice principal, not Michael Jordan, the basketball player. Mr. Jordon lived a block or so from my house. He was a great African-American guy. There was a beautiful young African-American woman who was one of my teachers, freshman year. She was as pretty or prettier than Halle Berry. When Mr. Jordon met her, he immediately telephoned his son who was a teacher in Michigan. His son came to visit Chicago and Mr. Jordon set them up on a date. They got married a year later. Now he has a beautiful daughter-in-law. Mr. Jordon would not put up with anyone's shit. My parents got to know him and thought a lot of him especially since he knew bullshit when he saw it.

My grade point average went from a three point something to a one point something. I started arguing with my parents at home. They knew I was constantly B.S.ing and not trying at all. My parents felt like I was getting uncontrollable. I understand now what they meant and why they did what they did. But then I just continued with the *wall* and the I just do not give a fuck attitude. So, I was sent back to Maryville. Fuck it. Lost that hand.

I went to Nipper high school near Maryville. I could have gone to Hersey High School, a good high school in Des Plaines, but I did not want to put in the effort. Nipper was a school for dummies. "Okay, fuck it, I don't even care no more, whatever, I really don't really care". I will go to the easy dumbass school and act like a dumbass. I will fly through the school and just bullshit them around and get out of school early. It was the same curriculum as Hersey and I got a Hersey High School diploma. Now some days, I think to myself, you had a chance to go to Hersey, a high ranking high school in Illinois. I also could have stayed at Lincoln Park High School with my friends, but I opted to be with a bunch of dumbasses all day at Nipper. Not the brightest move.

I thought I had the upper hand and was great at manipulating everyone else. I was controlling people and the system. But now I realize, it was not to my benefit. I thought I was winning at cards, but I was doing nothing to improve my chances or make things better. You should really learn to work it and manipulate things to your own benefit, not do things that will slow you down and hurt you in later life.

In July of the year 2000, my oldest half-brother, Avery, was gunned down by rival gang members. He was 19 and standing on a corner, when he was shot numerous times and died. Here is part of his obituary that is a warning that I should have taken heed of when I was younger.

"Avery like so many of our head-strong unprepared young black boys of today was determined to live life "his way" and so he did. He thought he knew all the answers......he thought himself smart, fast and clever – and for a few short years he was that......Avery was not infallible, as proven on the night of July 20th, when his young life was snuffed out on the streets of familiar ground (with his brother Daniel at his side) ...... If Avery's life meant anything to you....... learn from his mistakes. Your changed and better life can only give honor and purpose to Avery's senseless and premature death".

I am a lot like Avery. I went to the funeral. It was pretty much a blur. Relatives and other strange people I did not know kept coming up to me and saying things about my brother and mother I did not want to hear and asking me questions I did not want to answer.

I was still going home to the O'Connors on the weekends. One time the van was picking me up and several Maryville residents asked if they could come into use the O'Connor's bathroom. Holly was sitting at the kitchen counter eating fruit and chatting with the people who came in to use the bathroom. One of the younger kids, Derrick Thurman, from my Maryville house came and sat down at the counter and started chatting up Holly, telling her what a lovely house she lived in. It turns out later that he becomes my foster brother. I previously told Holly and Paul in jest, but not really in jest, that they could not get any more foster children and Miles agreed with me. We did not want to share them.

Since Derrick was one of the residents of the house I lived in at Maryville, I knew him well and I knew he was a nice kid. Derrick was in a similar situation that I was in, when I was younger. He had an older half-brother at Maryville. Maryville had tried to place them together in a foster home, but Derrick's older brother was angry and difficult to place. So, they decided to split up the half-brothers. Paul was talking to Brian White, who was in charge of my Maryville home. Brian was telling Paul what a nice kid Derrick was and how he needed a home. Paul wanted to take on some more children and told Brian he'd have to talk to Holly. I told Paul they could become foster parents to Derrick, but he was the last one.

Paul kept talking about taking on more foster children, because he thought we had it too easy. I was a partner at Arthur Andersen at the time and I didn't think we had it too easy. I was working 10 to 12 hours a day. Also, kids of any kind are very stressful, especially ones like Joel. I had enough stress with Miles, Joel and work.

I did say to Paul one day out of the blue, that I wouldn't mind taking on a kid like Derrick who stopped in the house that day. He was bright and had an amazingly sophisticated sense of humor. I could tell in just the few minutes I met him. It wasn't until several months later, that Paul spoke to Brian. Paul came home and told me about Derrick needing a home. I couldn't say no. That's how we ended up with our third son, Derrick.

I went to the Nipper School for the spring semester and then to summer school because I was still farting around. I got my first job working at

Champs Sports, in the Randhurst Mall near where I lived at Maryville, in Des Plaines, Illinois. It was perfect for me because I still loved sneakers, especially Michael Jordan's. I was good at selling. I always knew you had to make people comfortable with their purchase. I had the gift of gab at an early age. I did not want to sell something to people that they did not like or that I would not actually invest in myself. I had to believe in the product. I had an instinct for people and knew the products. I am sure I could sell anything if I believed in it. I understood supply and demand.

I knew what people wanted. I was a Nike-head all my life. Nike was hot at the time. I especially loved the "Just Do It" attitude and slogan. It is like the coolest thing you can ever come across in your life in the fast lane. I interpreted it as "do what you want to do". Live your life as you want to do. Just do something and not really think about the consequences. That was me.

I am selling a lot of shoes and making a paycheck. I also got a discount on the new Jordan's that came in, so I could buy way more pairs of shoes. I was still going home on the weekends. I am now going into my senior year. That fall I had so many credits and really did not need to go to school after the fall session. When December was over, I decided with the people at Maryville, that I would graduate with the class in May, but I did not have to go to classes. I ended up just working and that was great for me. I was also taking a class at the local junior college. That was boring.

Then something happened at Champs. My manager had some kind of emergency family issue and stormed out of the store. Right then and there I took control of the store. I pretty much knew how to do everything. There were new Adidas, Mercedes CLR shoes coming on line. I put a pair on my feet, because we were supposed to sell them. It was a great running shoe. The manager of the store was a lot older than I was and he neglected the store. When he returned two weeks later, I got fired. I did not understand any of the reasons that they gave me. I thought I made the store. I was bumped up to a supervisor position at 16 or 17 years old and should have been made a manager.

I found out later that Foot Locker was owned by the same people that owned Champs. I should have gone for a manager position there. I was always good at sales because I was always able to talk and sell to the customers. I can do a lot of things but was never able to put them together with someone who gave me a chance. I asked God why he blessed me with the gift and the curse, meaning that I thought I had the ability to do it, but you can never get the position.

My life goes on. I try different jobs throughout my life and I got through whatever job I wanted to. It was an important thing for me working various jobs, here and there. I worked at White Castle on the night shift sometimes, sometimes not. I was making a check and still doing what I wanted to do until I had to graduate.

Maryville at the time was a good place. It was run by Father Smith who really cared about kids. I do not know where I would be without him. I had my ups and downs at Maryville because of the disciplinary system. I felt that I was grown and did not need to follow their stupid rules. There were also some great people running my house. Brian, a very caring person, was in charge of the House. TC, a large African-American was there at night. I had fights with them all and loved them all. I still really did not understand what it was like to be a man. They all helped me make it through another chapter of my life. There were also a few lazy people there who did not care much.

The Duke basketball coach, Mike Krzyzewski's niece, Jamie, was the girls' basketball coach. She was lots of fun to be around and I got to meet her uncle. Maryville was a big place where a lot of good and some bad stuff went on, just like the streets where I grew up on the Southside. I met a lot of cool kids from every gang in Chicago and I really liked them. Everyone was in the same situation. Everybody was cool. I learned there that nobody situation is better than anyone else's. I am not better than anyone else and I never claimed to be. I just put myself in that bracket GDI, God Damn Individual. I usually did not get treated like a GDI. Many people tried to put me down. But no one holds you down but yourself, at the end of the day. You must understand that in life.

In 2002, I graduated with a diploma from Hersey High School in Des Plaines. Since I got my high school diploma, the Department of Children and Family Services, supported me until I was 21 years old. I was supposed to be going to school and/or working. I had my own apartment on the south side of Chicago. I applied and got accepted to the Chicago Art Institute. I could have gone to university but did not go, because I felt that it would just be a waste of time. I would have just gone there and partied. But that was what I was doing in Chicago while I was at art school. I had no oversight. I was still doing whatever I wanted to do, and I knew that it was not good for me. I met up with a woman named Inga who I hung out with. She braided my hair into cornrows, another vanity of ghetto life. I thought I was all that with my own place and being in school. I went into a free fall, learning to be even more of an asshole than I already was. I still think I am kicking it at the time.

My girlfriend at the time was Courtney. She ended up getting pregnant. I had another girlfriend at that time that I also got pregnant. The two women were friends and were both very unhappy with the situation. Courtney got me alone in the LaSalle School playground, pepper sprayed me and tried to beat me with a baseball bat. Both women did not have their babies. I told Paul about Courtney's abortion. He was totally upset because he is pro-life. It will hurt him to read this.

Usher had the song "Confessions" at the time I got the women pregnant:

> "Everything that I've been doing is all bad
> I got a chick on the side with a crib and a ride
> I've been telling you so many lies
> Ain't none good, it's all bad
> And I just wanna confess
> It's been going on so long........."
> Usher 2004

This was my confession at the time also, so I thought I was cool, but everything was really crashing down on me. I still had my head up my ass. I now realize that sex and having babies are so different from having a loving wife, family, and children. I could not have known that growing up in the environment I did, with no one really caring about me.

I started skipping classes and failing classes at art school, so I switched to Culinary Arts at the Cordon Bleu Chicago. I lived on 47th and Ellis at that time and I thought it was great, but you know I was getting ready to become 21 years old and had no direction. This is the hood, I got to know a lot of women. I sold drugs to get more money. I did not prove to be any better at Culinary Arts than Fine Arts, since I did not go to classes and did not try. So, I am falling off at school, not doing well in any of my courses.

Joel kept telling us he was going to Culinary Arts classes. His answers to questions about the school were not quite believable. One night he said he would cook for us. He made us linguine alfredo. We all said how good it was. Two days later I found an empty jar of Prego AlFredo Sauce in a corner of one of our cabinets. He could have at least but it at the bottom of the trash under some other garbage, so it did not stink up the kitchen.

He tried to come back to live in our house one time. I was against his coming. Paul talked me into it. Paul and I ended up agreeing that he could stay if he followed the house rules. We wrote out a list of ten rules and told him if he broke any of them he had to pack up and leave

- *No alcohol*
- *No drugs*
- *Nobody in the house with him when we weren't there*
- *No stealing*
- *Stay employed*
- *No lies*
- *Clean up after himself*
- *Love himself and others*
- *Try to improve himself by educating himself*
- *Treat everyone with respect*

He came back to live in our house on the Sunday before Thanksgiving. Paul was out of town. I was working. Joel called me at work and asked if I was going to the gym after work. I said yes because I was planning to, but I could usually tell when Joel was up to something. I decided to go straight home from work. When I got there, he was in the basement drinking with some girl. He had been at home only three days and had broken three rules in one evening. I told him to pack his things and leave. He tried to babble some excuses, but I said leave. I was not an idiot or a sucker.

By now, I should have figured out how to do the right things. But for me, there was no other way but to do these things and keep making the same mistakes over and over. You are young, and you are dumb so that is all you want to do anyways just keep living your life at age 21 with all the freedom in the world. Someone else is paying and you have just no parental guidance. I messed up and it ended up biting my ass.

My parents moved me to 530 West Arlington Place which is down the street from their house, about 15 minutes away. I loved the studio apartment, but I just continued doing reckless and dumb stuff that many people did at that age. I was still seeing Courtney even after the mace and baseball bat incident. She ended up getting pregnant again and decided to keep the baby.

My dad wanted me to join the U.S. Marines. I kept putting it off for years. I took the test twice and failed it on purpose. After you take the test and fail it twice you need to wait a certain amount of time before you can take it again. I knew the guys at the Recruiting Office for years before I got in. Sergeant Vasquez was the guy who got me in. He was a small Mexican-American recruiter who became my friend. He never pressured me to join. I started training with him and he convinced me to do more with my life. I turned 23 years old, had a baby on the way. I knew my life was going nowhere. I was working at Marshall Fields. I was still hustling on the side. I was not happy with myself. I took the test a third time and passed it. I was going to wait until the baby was born and go in to the Marines at the end of June.

Having thrown Joel out of the House, a couple of times already, I told Paul that Joel could move back home once he was accepted into the Marines and had a scheduled start date. One day when I walked in the door from work, my older son Miles told me he was accosted right in front of the house by some gang member's driving by in a car. They said, "Are you Joel's brother" Miles said yes, and they responded, "Tell your brother we know where he lives, and he better watch himself.

I put up with a lot over the years and tried my best to have self-control. I know how to swear, because I grew up in New Jersey. I tried not to swear at home and work, not wanting to set a bad example. At that moment, I went berserk. I sent Miles to find Joel, who was playing dice over on Orchard Street, at a housing project. When Joel walked in the door, I pointed my finger at him and said something like, "YOU STUPID MOTHERFUCKER!!! WHAT THE HELL ARE YOU DOING? YOU FINALLY GET ACCEPTED TO THE MARINES AND HAVE A BABY ON THE WAY. YOU CALL UP THE RECRUITING OFFICE AND GO IN THE MARINES TOMORROW. YOU STUPID MOTHERFUCKER, YOU ARE NOT GOING TO GET SHOT OR ARRESTED IN CHICAGO BEFORE YOU GET INTO THE MARINES............" I went on for about twenty minutes. I was more afraid of Joel getting shot in Chicago than in Iraq.

When Paul came home from work. I immediately told him the story. Paul went to Joel and started a similar rant to mine. "YOU IDIOT...". After Paul finished, Joel said to him, "I already called Sergeant Vasquez and I am leaving for Boot Camp on Monday. It was the only time Joel ever really listened to me.

There were people that knew I was going to get in trouble "cuz I'm from Chicago you can't tell me nothing". Some things in life are meant to be challenged and changed. If people do not challenge the status quo, it leaves room for people just to keep doing what they are doing. My dad kept challenging me to be a better person. I always wanted to debate everything because debating something means you must go back and forth. But if you do not know your facts, you could be wrong. There are times when you should just sit there and agree. I decided to leave early for the Marines.

Chapter 5

Early morning on May 2, 2005, my staff sergeant called to tell me to get ready to leave. The Marines were going to pick me up from home to take me to a hotel. The following day a group of us new recruits would be leaving for San Diego. I got ready and all my family was sitting on the front stoop with me to wait for the Marines to come pick me up. My pregnant future wife, Courtney, was there. Paul and Holly were there. We were all just looking at each other. I was not really nervous. It was like moving from house to house and family to family all over again and I was used to being put in different situations. I looked at my mom and I can see how she is nervous. My Dad, he is calm and everybody else's looking trying to understand why I am leaving before the baby was born. I kissed everyone good bye and that is when I knew things were going to change.

We were actually happy to see Joel go. We originally thought he should stay around until his baby was born. But when we saw he was still hanging out with a bad crowd, we were more worried about him being arrested, than we were that he would be shot in Iraq.

A month or so before I was excepted into the Marines, I got a call one day from a relative who says he knows that my birth father is in Chicago. He was apparently living in Mississippi most of my life. I went with Miles to see him. He was in a wheelchair in a veteran's home on the south side of Chicago. When we got inside Miles easily picked out my father. Miles told me my father's face looked just like an older version of me. It was very awkward, and I really did not want to have anything to do with him. My father had a picture in his room of him when he was in the Marines looking just like me. I had no idea that he was in the Marines. The picture of me from the Marines when I am in my dress blues, looks exactly like his picture. I have them both and you cannot really tell us apart.

I left with the Marines and we went to a hotel in the suburbs. I met some new Marine candidates also making the trip to San Diego. Some of these were large women. I was in good shape having gone to the training with the people from the recruiting office. I was thinking to myself, that these large women are not going to make it to the Marine Corps and how did they pass any of the tests to get in. I started getting to know the women and tried to help them out. I thought this is cool because it is like you can help somebody out without trying to hit on them.

I could not sleep that night because we were leaving the next day. I hung out with some of the other recruits and got back to the room at four o'clock in the morning. I took a shower and started getting ready for tomorrow. I fell asleep and woke up to be on time to meet the others at 8 a.m. I looked at myself in the mirror and said, "hey, this is what it is". I was physically prepared. I was not sure about being mentally prepared, but I thought I could take what they could dish out.

We all met in the morning and checked in at eight o'clock with the staff sergeant. Other master sergeants are there. We got on the bus and headed for the airport to fly to San Diego. It was a long-ass flight. I have been in airports a lot of times and I have been through security checks. I thought this should be nothing. But, by the time I got to San Diego I had that choked up feeling in my throat. I really could not talk or eat because I knew that everything was about to change. Everybody else was sitting at McDonald's eating Big Macs. I was just sitting there drinking a pop. Then, I tried to call my parents. I started talking to people to get change to make the call because I did not have my cell phone. Now I see all other people from the military arriving. There were all these young kids. Most are around 20 years old. I was 23 at the time and I am looking at the kids and thinking that they have no idea what life is like.

Then everyone is told to line up and get on the bus. As we got on the bus, they told us to put two hands on our knees and look down. I am thinking, what type of shit is this, what do you mean look down, why am I looking down at the ground, this is retarded. It turns out that they did not want us to see the base yet. When we get there, there is all types of fuckery going on and what I mean by fuckery means is that they are all playing games with us. They were teaching us to "unfuck ourselves" by testing us. So, there is a lot of fuck-fuck games about to go on. So, we pull up, I am really nervous and some of the guys are crying. It is the weirdest fucking thing I have seen in my fucking life. The drill sergeants got on the bus and they broke all hell. That is what they are supposed to do. I mean they said. "Hey now you get to fuck up. Welcome to the motherfucking United States Marine Corps Recruit Depot San Diego".

People did not know how to act. Me, I was laughing because I knew they were going to be yelling in my face. My dad did that very often. I was about to start laughing. They are yelling, "get off the bus, get off the bus, get off the bus, get off the bus, line up on the square, line up on the shoes, line up on the footprints". They had footprints painted on the ground where you were supposed to stand and line up for the intake. I was laughing along with a couple of other people from Chicago. We were from the streets; the urban life and we knew what was happening. It was 10 a.m., when we arrived in San Diego. Now it is about 7 p.m., 1900 military time. Then they make us walk through this door and that is when your life gets snatched from you. You are a civilian all the way in and they need to unfuck you.

The first stop is the barber shop. I am from the city where haircuts count and already had a very low haircut. These cocksuckers tried to cut my hair again. I told them, "You are not touching my damn hair, You are not scalping my head when it is already cut low as hell." I was surprised that they passed on making me have my hair cut. There were other guys crying because their hair got cut off. I am sitting there laughing again. Then they take you to another room. It is like an underground jail type setting where you are going through tunnel after tunnel. It was like visiting Tim in the maximum-security jail in Wisconsin. Then, you have all types of people coming in there talking to you. I was thinking that this is like really nothing. You have to strip your clothes off. Then, they start giving you clothes. You are leaving your old life behind you to get ready for what they have in store for you.

So now it is probably about 1 or 2 in the morning and we head over to our barracks. It was like a big squad bay with a gang of Marines. We were going to be there for like 3 or 4 days. We were in training and classes, learning the rules and where things were. I am on my way to the barracks. I got yelled at because I was laughing. One guy would not shut up. I told the guy, stop fucking talking to me. It is now about 3:30 in the morning and this guy keeps running his mouth. The guy was a sergeant. I told him again, "shut the fuck up, stop talking to me". That is when all hell broke loose. He grabbed me by my shirt and threw me one way and I came back the other way. I knew he was supposed to put me in my place. This time I knew things were real in the field.

They were not about to put up with any shit from us and I decide I am not going to play any shit with them.

So welcome to the barracks. We start making our racks up. About four in the morning, it is chow time. They take us to eat. Everybody else wants to eat, but I could care less about food at four o'clock in the morning. I am more concerned about drinking some Pepsi. I was trying to drink a Pepsi and eat a donut. Again, I had the feeling like when you want to talk and say something, but you cannot because it stuck in your throat. I was like more choked up because I did not know what was about to happen. So, we are at the chow hall and we are lined up all crazy just like an old school cafeteria. There are 50 to 200 guys lined up outside standing by each other getting ready for chow at 4:30 in the morning. Guys start eating whatever and however they want. Nobody bothered anybody during the first four days about how or what you ate. I was so choked up, I did not want to eat. I was sleepy, and I knew they were just trying to torture us. They take us back to the squad bay and we still have not been to sleep.

We go to classes for the next couple of days. We are all fatigued but starting to get to know each other. We learn about the history of the Marine Corp. I am still acting like this is a joke. Later, I look around and look at all the other Marines who are in the second month or final phase of the Marine boot camp and think they are cool. I start seeing myself as a Marine.

The Marine Corps boot camp is the longest and toughest boot camp of any of the Military Services. I am not trying to put down the Army, Airforce, and Navy but I believe that everyone put into military service should be put through Marine training. The Marine Corps has higher standards. They are not training you just to survive as a soldier, but they are training you to survive as a killer. I had killing instincts. That is the difference between the Marines and everyone else, we are trained to kill. This always stuck in my head.

We have been up for twenty-four hours. They explained to us the reasons why we must stay awake. So, as class is going along you are learning more things about the Marine Corps. We head back around 18:00 that night. Then we went off on our way to the chow hall again to eat dinner. This is the first time I have seen a drill instructor walk across the table. I was sitting there minding my own business. We are supposed to sit there at the table with two feet on the floor and straight knees. They tell you when you can eat. So, they tell us to eat and I know what is about to happen. They told us not to get any sweets on our trays. One guy does not listen and ends up putting some sweets on his tray. The sergeant gets on the table and tells everyone they have to get up from the table. We were all excused from the table before we could eat. The drill instructor ran across the table yelling, "you get the fuck off the table, get the fuck off the table right now. You disgust me, get off the table". I was laughing, but some were crying about not being able to eat any food.

I understand why the sergeant did that. They were trying to make us see that you are only as strong as your weakest link. So, I understand that you need to make your weakest link strong. We get back to the squad bay and a couple of guys got mad at the guy who put the sweets on his tray and wanted to beat him up. I stopped him from getting his ass whooped. I am telling them, "leave the man alone, we have to get through this shit together". I am starting to realize that we are brothers, but brothers tend to fight with each other.

Finally, at 21:00 we got to go to sleep. I am sitting in my bed thinking this shit is not real. I look skinny. All of us had shaved heads and were looking skinnier. I think it is cool that we are all looking the same. I am one of the few African Americans. I love that they put everybody on one level, nobody is higher, nobody is lower. This is where brotherhood starts for me in the Marine Corps.

We wake up on Thursday. We got a little sleep, but we were up early at 04:00. We have to get ready for the Physical Training ("PT") test. The PT test is to see what physical abilities you have in order to place you in a specific training program. We run half a mile, do pull-ups and crunches and that is the end dock before you have to go to your squad or company late that Friday. We all stretch before the training. I am ready to run, and I am going to knock this shit out of the park. I did 100 crunches and I did the 20 pullups. I did the run and got a good time. It was hot, but I got a First-Class rating on the personal fit test. I never got anything lower. So, Thursday ended on a great note for me.

Friday is called Crossing Over when you get assigned to your Company. Everyone is alphabetically ordered Alpha, Bravo, Charlie, Delta, etc. I was assigned to Fox Company. Now we are ready to go up north to Camp Pendleton. We had a lot of packing to do and we got specific instructions on how to pack. We took the train. We had to get mentally prepared for hiking. For two weeks we had a routine. Of course, being who I am. I am having some problems with the guys in the platoon and I do not understand why the drill instructors are acting the way they act. So, it came to a point where I knew that they could not break me. At the end of the day these guys were trying to help me out and I am being stupid not realizing this. I was trying to fight against them and I was not very smart at doing that. Later on, in life, I learned that you cannot fight against everybody that is trying to help you.

So, we are heading to Camp Pendleton on Sunday night. The next day we start on the hike. It is a three-mile hike and I am seeing some weak shit from some of the other guys. They are falling and complaining. I am ready to go, but you have to go on their time and at their pace. The purpose of this training is to get ready for the crucible which is the biggest step in Phase 2. You have to pass the crucible to get your Eagle Globe and Anchor medal. You learn to use the rifle during this time, how to shoot and how to break it down which I thought was fascinating. The process is very detailed, and you must be meticulous about it. It is hot outside. They put you under a tent and drill you all day long. I am acting up in class. I would rather get hazed than sit there all day.

I thought everybody knows how to shoot a gun. Not true. It was difficult at first. We had to learn to shoot standing, kneeling, and prone. There are thirty or forty people lined up and you must pay attention on how you hold your weapon. Lots of rules. Treat, treat, never keep, keep was one saying we learned. Treat every weapon like it is loaded. Keep your fingers off the trigger unless you intend to shoot. You have to qualify to use fire arms within the second or third week of training.

One day I am on the range learning to shoot. I start to get into it with one of the staff sergeants from another platoon. He told me to do something, and I said, "who the hell are you talking to. I ain't your child". He said come here Riley, go away Riley and he pushed me, so I pushed him back. All the other instructors saw the commotion. Imagine five or six drill instructors yelling in your face, spitting at you, and telling you that you ain't shit". I could not do anything about it. But I just sucked it up because I realize that we are just playing a game. I am still playing cards and I think I am ahead. They all decided to make my life a living hell for the next week.

When we got to qualifying day, I am tired from all the hazing. I ended up causing my platoon to lose becoming the head platoon. Getting ready for the crucible you go through a lot of drills through obstacles, and live fire to learn various tactics and jungle warfare. Marines have to be prepared for land, air, and sea.

One part of the training involves pugil sticks. A pugil stick is a heavily padded pole-like training weapon. It is about fifty inches long and is used by military personnel in training for rifle and bayonet combat. You get to fight people that you do not like. I have a lot of anger built up. They put me against some big guys, they would hit me, and I always thought I was fine because I got back up. I beat the hell out of some of the kids. I always got back up. The drill instructors were still mad at me for getting in their face.

So, two days before the crucible they hazed me all day. I did not get any water all day. The first two people I beat. When the third bout came around. I got dehydrated and passed out. They knew what they were doing. They stuck a thermometer up my ass and threw all kinds of ice and water on me. That is how they got even with me. I knew it and I was like whatever motherfuckers.

So, now I am thinking that I am switching games. It is now the Riley games. I got better and rested a couple of days and got back on line to get ready for the crucible. For the crucible you get up at three o'clock in the morning and start hiking. By five o'clock in the morning you have reached the first destination to get ready for a fifteen-mile hike up a hill called "The Reaper". It was really beautiful, and

I was having fun. I was prepared and was helping other people by dragging them up the mountain. I never thought my legs would give out on me, so I am charging the hill. That is where you get your Eagle, Globe, and Anchor Medal. The emblem stands for the three areas the Marines serve "On Land, In Air and On Sea". After you get an Honor, Courage, and Commitment Medal. It has an amazing effect on you.

You come back down the mountain and have the biggest meal of your life for making it through the grueling day. I was able to complete everything. It was cool, and I felt it in my heart. I now thought honor, courage and commitment meant something. Now we get ready for phase three.

That night I got into a fight with the same kid that I did before. This time we are cleaning up and trying to prepare to head back. He got all smart mouthed and called me a nigger. He had a mop in his hand. I said to him, "what did you call me". He said, "I called you a nigger". I took the mop from him and smacked him in the face with it. Then I took his head and pile-drived it into the ground and took my legs and started kicking him.

I got disciplinary action and got sent back a week and had to join a different company. I had to redo the gas chamber exercise, but they did not make me redo the crucible. The new company was called

Lima. They found out that I was a hard ass and a smart-ass kid from Chicago. They gave me a hard time and I got used to it.

We had about a month left at this time. We have more drills and training. Then we have to turn in our guns and get fitted for uniforms. There was a lot of physical training. I made it good with my staff sergeant and my sergeant because I was the type that would rather get hazed than miss the action. So, every time someone would do something that required doing push-ups or other physical activity, I was like take me, take me. I earned their respect. Things are getting better. You know how to wear a uniform better. You really feel personal gratification. I have figured out the PT thing. I made myself run on my tippy-toes, so I was always fast and smoked everyone in all the platoons. They made me race against everyone in the platoon. They knew I would win the race and the sergeants would bet money on me, on the sidelines. I loved them for that. It was the coolest thing to know we had some really good guys.

So, it is about time to graduate from boot camp. We do final drills in our uniforms. During the last week people are allowed to put on their clothes that they came in with. It is awesome to watch all the people who have lost weight and their clothes are way too big. These final drills are called the fashion show because everybody looks and feels better about themselves. It was very cool. After being in the military, I can teach anyone how to lose weight. Next you start preparing for parade day and going home. Everyone is calling people and making reservations.

On parade day all the parents come to see you graduate. Everyone is nervous. Right before the parade, my old staff sergeants came in and said, "Whether or not you know it, you have the ability to lead and follow. We just tested you and we knew that you would never give up on yourself. You have our utmost respect". I learned at once that I could be a leader or a follower in the Marines. In my head, I always wanted to control things and play the game the way I wanted to play it.

There is a morning run on the parade deck. I did not have to run because I had screwed up my foot. The parade was great, with lots of friends and family cheering. Graduation was the best seeing my family, Holly, Paul, Derrick, Miles came along with my wife and newly born son. My son, Justin was born on Father's Day June 19th. Some friends of the family also showed up, Randy, and Rudy, the husband of Marge. Marge was the one who coached baseball with Paul and Holly and looked after me when I first came to their house. It was a cool thing. I got to spend the evening with them. The next day we all left to go back to Chicago. I was not really prepared to be a dad. It was still a great feeling.

Parade day was something special for all of us. Before the parade they have all kinds of show and tell meetings with the parents and family members. They take you to various places around the base and show you videos and talk about what the recruits went through and what it means to a family member of a Marine. The base in San Diego is quite spectacular. After the third or fourth video or speech. I said to Paul, they have repeated the same things over and over, I think they are trying to brainwash us and prepare us for the possible death of our children". It makes sense. Paul thought what I said was terrible.

During the morning of parade day, all the recruits do a run around the parade route for all the family members to see. We keep watching all the various companies of men go by. We all keep looking for Joel. In all of the groups of hundreds of people there were only about five African-Americans. We thought we should easily be able to pick out Joel. But he was nowhere to be seen. All of us were panicking because we are thinking, oh no Joel has screwed up at the last minute – his old self sabotage. We knew about him getting put back a week because he was fighting.

Later it is time to go to the parade ground and sit in the stands. When we sit down Miles has us all say a prayer that Joel is okay and will be graduating with his platoon today. I think we all had been praying since the morning run. Finally, the parade starts, and we are still nervous. Many companies parade by and line up in formation, and no Joel. My stomach was in knots. When we see him, I believe in the last company coming in, we are all thrilled and proud. Joel looks great. He walks, talks and acts like a proud new Marine.

After the parade in the evening, Paul, Joel, Miles, Derrick, Courtney, and Justin sat down at one of the tables outside on the campus as the sun was going down. The weather was just perfect outside, warm with a light breeze. I remember saying how thankful I was at having such a great family. It was one of the best times of my life.

Holly, Paul, Derrick, Joel, Miles, & Courtney
At Graduation From Bootcamp

Chapter 6

I flew home with the family to Chicago after graduating from boot camp. I was really fit and proud in my uniform. I wore my uniform to church on Sunday and an older gentleman palmed me a $100 bill. I liked the attention. After being home a couple of weeks, I had to fly back to Camp Pendleton. Everyone came with me to the airport. Holly and Courtney are crying. Holly tries to upgrade me to first class, but I refuse, saying I am only going to be sleeping, don't waste the money. I say goodbye to my son and everyone else.

I am going back to Marine Combat Training which lasts about six weeks. The first week you get into your barracks and they present you with a curriculum, which is a list of all of the things you need to do and learn over that time period. For example, each day we would have a different length hike such as 2k, 3k, 0r 5k hike and then a 15k hike and then some other type of training, like artillery training. I am all pumped up because I am thinking this is going to be easy until we are told we are going to be carrying heavy artillery. Heavy artillery includes, M16 rifles which are about 40 inches long and weight 7.5 pounds loaded, M240 rifles which are about 50 inches long and weight around 25 pounds and Mk 19 grenade launchers that are 43 inches long and weigh 72 pounds unloaded, along with ammunition. We also must carry our backpacks. We get detailed instructions on how to pack up our back-packs, so you are prepared for any type of weather. Packs include, thermals, boots, and extra socks. Socks are the most important because no matter where you are going your feet get cold or hot and sweaty. Socks prevent your feet from getting messed up down the line.

Today everybody must stage up for the first hike. Stage up means getting together the whole battalion to prepare for the mission. We are off on the first 2k and I am walking out in front of the pack. I like walking out front because the people are faster. But as a marine you can't go too far ahead because you have to make sure everyone is together. I like to be in the front or in the back hurrying up people. The middle is for people who are dragging, and you must hurry them up also. I thought we were going to hike on flat land, but we start going up into the hills. It is hot outside. I was doing fine but as a Marine you need to fall back and help everyone out. I kept carrying my brothers from the back and bring them up to the front to keep the guys on the move. I would grab someone's pack or rifle to give them a break. Sometimes they would physically lean on me. I felt useful and that what I was doing had a purpose.

After the hike, all the brothers started talking to each other. We all wanted to get to know each other and where everyone comes from. A few of the guys started making all kinds of slick remarks to each other. There were a couple of black guys there that I knew from Chicago. Some guys from Texas started calling us niggers. The word nigger gets brought up too much and everybody uses it. We are all supposed to be brothers, so this pisses me off. I don't care if you are white, black, brown, Christian, Jewish, whatever, our brothers all bleed the same blood. One of the guys from Chicago, Tony got offended and beat one of the kids up. At first, I laughed at the situation and tried to deescalate the matter. I didn't see the point of arguing, since we are all trying to accomplish the same mission. However, me being me, I ended up getting into the matter with the Texan. It wasn't so much that he called me a nigger it was the way he said it. He said, "You are nothing, you may be wearing a Marine uniform, but you are still going to be a nigger". I ended up threatening him, saying, "I'll beat your ass", and tried to do so. Of course, he ran to higher ups to tell them I was threatening him, not mentioning that he was calling us niggers. I got a reprimand and a disciplinary action which delayed me getting the next rank. I was on probation for six months until I could move up. I took that as a light punch. The cards were stacked against me at the time. I should have known that before playing the game.

When you first start a job, the company teaches you most of what you should know to do the work. They teach you how to set up, do the breakdown, put together, use the computer system. It works the same in the Marines. In the Marines, the system is play the game and understanding who you are playing against. Somebody is always going to outrank you and belittle you because of the power of authority. There are always going to be great people and bad people. That's life. But, I understood that I had to play the game with their rules and questionable practices.

The staff and NCO were not really mad about it. I had extra duties added in. The officers told me, "Riley you have character and you can be a leader or a follower. If you are a leader people will follow you whether you are doing positive or negative things". At the time, I did not quite understand that. As we get into more chapters, I will tell you what I got out of it down the line.

The second week in we are getting ready for the 5K on Friday. We also get more education on all the weapons that we are going to use. That Wednesday we learn how to break down a M240 rifle. The weapon requires two people to operate. It has armor-piercing bullets. The bullets can penetrate through pretty much anything, walls, tanks, etc. We go through all the characteristics of the weapon, the trigger mechanism, the coils, the springs, how to properly clean and breakdown all of its components. You can really hurt someone handling it the wrong way. We also learn how to launch grenades and about their back-blast radius, so you don't end up blowing yourself up. The training was a great experience. You must have killer instincts to defend The United States of America. I signed up because people did before me and I respect them. On Friday we stage up for the 5k. Here I go. I am there up front with the Heads of the Battalion, the Lieutenant Colonel, the Gunnery Sergeant, and the First Sergeant. I was talking to them because I just got into trouble. They addressed me as a man and a marine. That is when I realized that in order to get respect you must give respect. I learned that you must adjust to people and treat them as you would want to be treated. We had a great conversation. The First Sergeant asked me "Riley, so what do you want to do with your life? " and I said, "I want to be Sergeant Major". He said "Why do you want to be Sergeant Major? I said, "why not? I think I could be a Sergeant Major and I know I could be a Sergeant Major. When you chase something, you should go for the top." I did not want to settle for being just regular.

We're getting ready for the 5K and the First Sergeant says, "Riley, are you going to lead the charge. I said "Yes Sir! First Sergeant! I started the same routine I started in the front. We are all gung-ho. After the first two miles I see a couple of Marines dragging. I start motivating them, get your ass up, no polite stuff in the Marines. I grab one the them and take his rifle and my rifle and we get into our cadence. Semper Fidelis, always faithful. When one man falls we tighten the rope to get everybody back on line.

We were going uphill, downhill. I tripped up a lot of times. If I hurt somewhere, it didn't matter because I kept pushing. One of the Marine sayings is, pain is only temporary. But, you can break. You need to know your body, so I kept pushing. I am a United

States Marine, I am going to push this body God gave me until I can't push it anymore. So, the walk was great. I had the feeling of brotherhood.

Next, we must prepare mentally and physically for the 15k, the motherfucker of all hikes. We have a GO (General Ordinance) night where we go to a huge open area and learn to shoot the M203 weapon. The M203 is a grenade launcher that can be attached to a rifle. It is designed to be effective at breaking through windows and exploding inside, blowing up doors, destroying bunkers, etc. We get put into teams to practice night operations with GPS. They give us a bunch of tasks to perform, navigating and finding people. I had trouble figuring out the grids but being with my Marine brothers they helped me figure it out.

There were some marines with me that were a lot smarter than I was, but of course as a brother they didn't make me feel any less smart. They teach you and don't mind answering my questions. That's why I love being with the brothers. We continue practicing missions and preparing for the 15K playing games and doing night hunts. We're having so much fun playing games. It is a job where we are getting paid to play games. We are not really thinking about real war situations.

For the 15K I decided to fall back so I could make sure the line doesn't break in the middle. It was a similar hike to the 5K up hill and downhill. This time, however, I am carrying the heavier M240 grenade launcher instead of my M16 rifle. The first 5 miles I was fine. I'm running uphill with it. I could have given it up at any time, but I was trying to see how far I could go. My shoulders started getting all hard and aching, but I continue to push on. I made it seven miles succeeding at my own personal mission. I knew I could do it. We all made it across the 15K. When we finish and we all eat and get rehydrated. I was tired and burned out like everybody else. But, it was a great feeling.

This part of the training was over. You feel good that you passed and you're getting ready to go into your specific career training. Career training lasts anywhere from 2 months to a year depending on what job you have chosen or what has been chosen for you. I got my itinerary and I was heading to Fort Leonard, Missouri for Motor T (Transportation) to become a vehicle operator. My friends were all sent to different places, like Pensacola, Florida, Lejeune, North Carolina and Miramar, California. Others were staying at Camp Pendleton. We were all talking and sharing information on our new assignments. I went to apologize to the kid I tried to beat up and said I was sorry I insulted him. I knew we had to form a brotherhood. He appreciated the apology. He apologized too, and I thought it was great because it was sincere. All I wanted was for him to understand was that we were bigger than all of that.

We flew out on Sunday for Fort Leonard Wood, Missouri, an army base located in the Ozarks. We flew from Camp Pendleton to Atlanta and then on to Fort Leonard Wood. I was like damn what the hell is going on because I didn't know it was an army base. We have to get in our dress uniforms. The dress uniform is very uncomfortable compared to our training clothes. It is all tight and stuffy. The army is a breeze compared to the Marines. They get weekends off even during boot camp.

We all need to learn about the school and the new command and where we are going to be stationed. I think it is funny because all the boys at Fort Leonard are country boys. They have been driving all kinds of vehicles since they were kids. I was a city boy, used to public transportation and my driving ability was not first rate. In Chicago, we had a very small garage off an alley and I kept scratching up my parent's cars trying to park them. Holly and Paul made jokes about me going into Motor T due to my terrible driving.

We have to learn to drive all of the motor vehicles, trucks, Humvees, jeeps, etc. We have two men to a room in the barracks. We meet new people and have physical training every morning. I run into this kid named Stephen Overton, I knew from Basic Training. He was a blue-eyed old country boy from Tennessee. He was left back because he hurt his foot. I hated him. He was a straight, gung-ho, suck-up, Marine, for real. I start having skirmishes with him. One weekend he told me I had to do barrack's duty. I had just done barrack's duty. I told him I was not doing shit. He called me a nigger and then started complaining to the higher ups because he was technically ahead of me. I told the higher ups that we were all grown men and he shouldn't be talking to me that way. I told them instead of doing paperwork, we should fight it out like men. We just stayed away from each other for a while.

We were in class all day long. The class leaders like me because I would sit in class with a pound of gummy bears. I ate them all day long to keep awake. We spent a lot of time in the classroom. We also trained for driving on simulators that were grueling. They would rock back and forth and shake. They were really rough on the body and on my hands. After class I'd play basketball and hang out in the barracks. After the month was over we get assigned our posts. East Coast, West Coast, Overseas? I requested the West Coast as my first choice. Who are the two-people going to Okinawa, Japan, to the 3rd Reconnaissance Battalion, Riley and Overton. Later, I came to have the utmost respect for Overton. I love him because if he had not been so hard on me I would not be the person I am today. He taught me how to lead and follow.

Now I am leaving Fort Leonard to go to Chicago before I go off to Japan.

Chapter 7

I get two weeks leave before I have to take off for Okinawa, Japan. I return home to Chicago to spend time with my son, Justin, his mother Courtney and the rest of the family. When I got home I got invited to the Marine Corp Ball in Chicago. I ended up going with my Marine Gunnery Sergeant, my Staff Sergeant and my First Sergeant.

November 19th, 2006, I head off to Japan. I fly from Chicago to Tacoma, Washington. It was a 23-hour flight from Tacoma to Mainland Japan. Here we go to a foreign country with different customs, traditions and courtesies. The only foreign country I had ever visited was Canada. Because I am used to being shipped around I am not nervous. I figure I can pick up what I need to know.

My buddies and I are in the Tacoma airport drinking. I am hoping to get on the plane and pass out for the entire trip. Here's where I learn that drinking and flying do not go together. Six hours after getting on the plane I wake up still intoxicated. That was the worst feeling. I was all dehydrated and needed water. I wanted to have some more drinks to put me to sleep for the duration. My friends and I were saying why did we do all those shots, why did we drink so much. Not a good idea, especially before a long flight.

We get to mainland Japan and get off. Customs goes through everything. We must wait. As marines, we all roll with the punches. More waiting and we finally get on a flight to Okinawa. We flew into Okinawa at night. It looked like Las Vegas, all lit up with neon signs, cartoons and billboards. It looked like it looks on television with Hello Kitty and lots of other crazy signs. We wait to get picked up and taken to the barracks. I run into my friend Fredrick Amos from ATL. I get to talk to him and then they show us around the base. My duty station was further up North, and I am not going to go there until the following week. We get instructions on the courtesies in Japan, what to do and not to do. They drive on the left side of the road. There are little mopeds and motorcycles always zooming all over the place. I am a defensive driver. The streets looked like a video game to me.

I arrived at my duty station with the 3rd Recon the 24th of November, right before the Thanksgiving holiday. We go to the barracks and they show us where the chow hall is. I am hanging with guess who, Overton, because we were the only ones we knew. Then we get to meet the Motor T heads and other Marines in the barracks. This is where I meet my future best friend, Auturo Gonzalez. I thought he looked like an angry Mexican-American. He is always angry about something. He was about the same size I was and meticulous in his appearance. Later I learn he is a fucking asshole, just like me. We would end up being best friends down the line and to this day, he is still my best friend. Over Thanksgiving a lot of people were spending time with their families. I spent Thanksgiving with Overton.

After getting through all the paperwork, medical and dental records at 3rd Recon, I get sent up to the motor pool which is up the hill from our barracks. I get introduced to Sergeant Scott, the Staff NCO in charge. He had two tours in Iraq. There were other men working at the motor pool with Sergeant Scott. They had all just gotten back from Iraq with all types of meritorious awards. There was one corporal, Cardona, that I didn't get along with. He was a good lead and a good Marine but was not mature enough. He was younger than I was and liked using his authority to push people around, which as you probably guessed by now, I did not appreciate. He did not like my attitude either and we got into a number of skirmishes. Cordova and I kept bumping heads. He went back to Sergeant Scott and told him I was being belligerent.

We are running around Okinawa practicing our driving, just following daily orders. We have to pass a separate driving test in Japan. I passed the driving test in Chicago the first time, but I was worried about the one in Japan. I got my license and then we had to go on runs all over Okinawa. You get sent everyday somewhere else and you go without asking questions.

Staff Sergeant Scott was angry with me because one day his wife called, and I answered the phone. I could not understand anything she was saying and kept asking her to repeat herself. This was after my first month in Japan. He came up to me and started chewing me out about disrespecting his wife. I am standing at attention and hoping he'll talk to me like a Marine with respect. Instead, he continues to chew me out. I got angry and could not keep my mouth shut. I said, "Who the fuck are you talking to?". Wrong card to play, I am still learning. I ended up apologizing and realized that Sergeant

Scott was trying to find out what was going on. He really helped me become a better Marine.

While I was in Okinawa I had quite a bit of training. I was assigned to motor pool with the 3rd Recon. But I never went through the official Recon training program at the School of Infantry at Camp Pendleton. These guys go through fourteen weeks of Marine reconnaissance training. The course is so brutal that only about half of the Marines survive. Even though I was motor pool, I was attached to 3rd Recon because I had high physical training scores. Being attached to 3rd Recon in Okinawa meant I trained with them.

Training with 3rd Recon meant was grueling. We did Run Swim Run which consisted of rounds of running down the beach on the sand, jumping in a pool and swimming laps, then running down the beach again. You had to keep doing rounds until someone tells you to stop. We were also dropped from helicopters into the water about a kilometer off shore with rifles and other equipment. They would drop each of us at different interval from the helo (a large troop transport helicopter) and we would have to swim to shore, run to meet up with the other swimmers at a specific destination and run some more.

We also trained for real combat situations. They had a model Iraqi town where we learned how to clear towns and houses. Clearing a town meant having a group of marines going down each side of the street with rifles pointed downward having residents leave their houses. We would be practicing looking for enemy and weapons. There are specific procedures for breaching places where the enemy or weapons are thought to be hidden.

We also had jungle training where we would walk in the rain and through wet marshy areas. Having clean socks saved my feet after days of marching. We learned how to do observations. We slept in trucks and on cots. We did helicopter trips and practiced setting up communication lines and antennae to keep in touch with our command center.

I learned to run at high altitudes in Okinawa. Being from Chicago that is flat as a pancake, I only ran most of my life at sea level. I had to learn how to control my breathing. This made me fast both above and close to sea level.

While I was in Okinawa we got weekends off. I made a great friend, Natomi, when I was there. I still talk to her today. She was about 40 years old when I met her. Her close friend was dating one of my marine buddies. She was divorced and had been married to a Marine. We would all go out together on the town. I used to bring along other guys from the base to show them around. Natomi nicknamed me O Samo, which she told me means "Big Daddy" in Japanese slang. She told me that she gave the name O Samo because I was always looking after everyone else in the crowd.

Natomi showed me all around Okinawa. She took me to some beautiful parts of the island that a lot of the other Marines didn't get to see. It turned out that she had relatives that were in the Yakuza family. Some members of the Yakuza family are members of a violent international drug gang. I found out people used drugs in Japan. I guess I was naïve. I never associated the Japanese people with drugs. There were places we would go that there were lots of drugs, mostly marijuana and cocaine. I did not partake of any of the drugs.

However, I did get into some serious trouble in Okinawa. One Saturday evening, several of us went drinking in Kintown, about thirty minutes away from our base. Kintown had a lot of bars where Marines hung out. I had a few drinks at the bar. There were some sergeants from another base. One of the sergeants was intoxicated and bumped into me. I let it slide. Then his girlfriend passed by me and bumped into me. I said to them, "Look man you could say excuse me or something like that". He was like, "I am a such and such, I am a sergeant". I said, "Who the fuck are you talking to?" He put his hands on me. I pushed him and said, "I'll beat your ass". I took a swing at him but didn't hit him. His girl tried to step in the middle. A bunch of MPs from the base across the road came and got me. I kept saying it wasn't my fault, but I was outranked. I tried to explain that he put his hands on me and I am a dam man and I am not going to let anyone put their hands on me. Of course, I was the loser in this one and got a battalion level NJP (Non-judicial punishment). I got my rank reduced to private, a reduction in pay and 60 days of restriction. Another case where I could have played that hand better. I did put in the extra work that I needed to.

While I am on restriction we are getting trained up to go to Iraq. New weapons training and clearance. I am on probation, but I am still a Marine. I am pissed off about it, because I can't go out on the weekends, and must do extra chores. It sucked, but as we are getting ready for Iraq, I am learning all kinds of new things. Some guys are lazy but come around. My trouble was with authority. Then, I was finally starting to understand what I needed to do.

We are finishing up training in Okinawa. I am doing well and behaving myself. We get two weeks of leave before we start our journey to Iraq.

The Cards I Was Dealt The Hand That I Played

Chapter 8

I had asked Courtney, the mother of my son, Justin, to marry me in August when I was to be back in Chicago on leave before going to Iraq. I formally proposed to her at Lawry's Prime Rib and Steak House Restaurant in Chicago at the end of a family dinner. We agreed to be married during my leave in August. Paul uncharacteristically agreed to be the wedding planner. Courtney's step-mother did the flowers. I was just told to show up on August 20. I did that and brought along my best friend Auturo.to be my best man. Everything went smoothly from my end. My dad was a complete wreck. He was so nervous that people wouldn't show. Courtney's mother showed up more than a half hour late. Courtney would not start the wedding until she came. I guess he had no idea how hard it was to plan a wedding. He got a lot greyer since I last saw him.

Derrick, Auturo, Joel and Miles at Joel's Wedding

A couple of days after the wedding I took off for Okinawa to prepare for the long journey to Iraq. In September, we take off for Kuwait. We fly half way around the globe. We are in the plane being Marines, just chilling with each other, not thinking about what is ahead. We are getting to appreciate each other. We spent approximately seven days in Kuwait waiting to get lifted to Fallujah our area of operation ("AO").

We are in Kuwait now, getting a lot of briefings. The US Army has pretty much control of the base. I am thinking that Kuwait is heaven. The facilities are outstanding. The guys are all playing basketball. There are weight rooms. There are all different types of restaurants. How come they are not doing the work of getting shot at? I found out that the guys are transitioned there or get stationed there. A lot of marines and other military personnel are coming through there, both to and from Iraq and Afghanistan as well as from other countries around the world. We are just waiting to get transported up to our AO. We are getting our weapons ready and boning up on training for the mission at hand. So finally, we get word we are going to Fallujah at 18:30 hours. We loaded on a chopper with heavy artillery weapons that can land in a combat zone.

We load and start flying. I don't know how long we were in the air because I wasn't really paying attention. Suddenly, we are told we need to do a combat landing. They didn't teach us what a combat landing was. Are we getting shot at? Apparently, a Rocket Propelled Grenade ("RPG") was shot up in the air at us. The ride was rough, and I am thinking, I haven't even gotten to see the ground and I am going to die. This is a terrible way to go. I might as well jump out of this dam thing. Everyone is saying prepare yourself, prepare yourself when we have a nice little crash. We thought the plane's engines were about to die. I thought, we are landing in the middle of a combat zone with a combat landing. Not much you can do about it. Isn't that crazy. My head was all over the place at the time. My life was going to get taken in an airplane. Forget adrenaline, this was something else, having anxiety and wanting to be free. You don't know if you landed right or got hit. My head was spinning but I was prepared.

We did the landing and got out. We went from the flight deck to the 3rd Recon battalion office headquarters' setup in Fallujah. We formed with our companies. I am off to the Motor T group. I hung out with the Motor T guys fixing vehicles, weaponry and mounting equipment for the weapons, for Mk 19s and Mk 240. During the first week I was there, I had to add heavy armor plates to the desert vehicles. We also went out to practice shooting.

I had not yet been there a week when some men from our battalion got a mission to go outside the gate. The men are about five klicks (five kilometers in military terms) away from our base and there is a big explosion. Soon after, sirens go off. Over the speaker comes, "we need blood, we need blood". That's when I knew the shit was real and I knew that this was going to be one of those times when you have to strap yourself together. You trained for this. You are a Marine. You are trained to kill and not to hesitate, do the job and get the job done and not make excuses about it. To myself, I am thinking this is crazy, but I am trained and ready for anything that comes my way. You have to accept death and realize that life can be taken at any time. This is what you signed up for.

Anytime someone dies in combat, everyone in the battalion attends the funeral. I had to attend seven funerals in one week in Fallujah. I never liked going to funerals back home. These funerals were different. These were your brothers, one day they are there and the next day they are gone. What are these guys dying for, to do a job that you get a fucking pat on the back for? You don't look at it like that. We are over here to do a mission.

I was attached to Bravo company. We went outside the gate to some neighboring cities looking for weapons caches and IEDs. You have to be alert and prepared at all times because you are responsible for your brothers and they are prepared to do the same for you. The decisions that you make can hurt the team or save the team. It is not the leaders that are leading you. It is the people who have been there and seen it, done it, lived through it and can make adjustments when needed, that can tell you what to do.

Joel in Iraq

Joel and Michael – Okinawa Roommates

Joel on Military Transportation

On one mission we took over a home at 3:30 a.m. We were told that weapons were being stashed there. We were there about 2 to 3 days. I drove the truck with a 50-caliber rifle ("50 Cal, for short) on top, did watch with my rifle over my shoulder and handled some communications. We did some missions from there and found IEDs, caches and took in some detainees.

In week three, the Bravo company gets detached from Fallujah to Ar-Rutba near the Syrian border. I did not understand what impact we were making to help the people and their families. We got a General's briefing from the generals and commandants. I knew it was going to be rough. I was on my way to Syria. I am leaving some of my closest friends. I call my parents and talk to them. It's hard because they ask you where you are and what you are doing? I can't tell them because everything is confidential. That's the way it has to be.

We would get calls from Joel in Iraq. It is always good to hear from him because you know he is alive and not injured. It is very hard to talk to him because you cannot ask him anything, so it is difficult knowing what to say. He would tell us he went north, and the weather was colder where he was. We would tell him about home and his son. We had his wife, Courtney and his son living with us for about a year when Joel was away.

Chapter 9

Now I am on my way towards the Syrian border We are traveling in a formation called sticks. It looked like the start of a NASCAR race. There are vehicles in front of me and behind me. This is a long sixteen hour plus journey that requires going through various parts of a number of Iraqi towns. We must stop to get fuel. A lot of crazy stuff happened. One time a car pulled up and attacked some of the vehicles in the formation. The car immediately got "exited out", which means the car and occupants are no longer on the earth because they threatened us. At times, Iraqis with guns would appear from the desert and start shooting at our gas tanks to try and blow them up.

When the Marines are in combat protecting the United States, we are not allowed to shoot unless fired upon. That's why I have trouble understanding politicians and why they don't mandate proper training for policemen. I know the police are generally good folks and try to do their best. They could avoid some of the killing by doing some military type training. Cops have different rules in different jurisdictions, but a lot of cops are not trained to shoot properly. We are taught were to aim to stop someone from getting away or kill when necessary. We do practice failure drills. A failure drill is a close-quarters shooting technique that requires the shooter to fire twice into the torso of a target and follow up with a more difficult head shot that, if properly placed, will instantly stop the target. The Marines are trained to shoot to kill, and we are also taught restraint. We also learn how to take down individuals without weapons. We were not allowed to engage the enemy unless they engaged us first.

Later, I was out on duty taking care of the vehicles. I hear shots fired and see some flames going up. My Staff Sergeant came around and told me to "mount down" (get out of the truck) to go on a security mission. So, we are going from house to house to look for the source of the explosion. As I was going back to my vehicle, some gas hit us. We all put our gas masks on as we were taught. We never found out what the gas was or how it affected us. Later, everyone appeared to be okay.

It was amazing going through the houses looking for weapons from the enemy. The families appeared to be so poor, but they would often have older guns encrusted with jewels or made with gold parts. Some of the Marines would pick up pieces of the smashed guns as souvenirs.

We were told we had to go out and take over a school at 3:00 in the morning. I often did not know why we were doing specific jobs. We were just following orders. We pretty much took over the whole town. We cleared out the school by eight o'clock the next day. Then, we had to move content and set up Hesco barriers, big wire mesh type barriers use to protect the base. All the time we are carrying our rifles and wearing flak jackets. It was hard work.

We wanted to set everything up to make it feel like home. We had some talented country guys in Recon. These awesome guys knew how to build showers, put in water supply lines and build walls. We sweep and set up cots. When we were finished it was about 11a.m. the same day. We had power, so we were able to make it look like a state of the art home. It was too cool because we built a lot of it from scratch. The work is challenging but it is satisfying.

We had to keep the place clean. We had to take the human waste outside and mix it with gasoline and burn it. I didn't mind. It was just a fire to me. Every day is a new journey. We continue to go on missions, both day and night. We hooked up with the army for missions. In November, the number of missions increased. We had many more with the army. In December, we had a lot of patrols. On Christmas we were on helicopter patrol on the Syrian Border. We were scheduled to be on the ground for six hours. One of the spark plugs on our helicopter went bad. We had to stand duty protecting the heli while waiting for a spark plug. I ended up spending Christmas on top of a cold snowy mountain near Syria. We were locked in, but we managed. We headed back down to a different base in Ar-Rutba. The base had a small chow hall and little workout room. The army had a set up for their laundry. We were assigned to a little trailer. Each branch of the military had their own trashy trailer park inside of a big huge trailer park. Every branch stayed in its own area. I ran into one of my friends. She was stationed there with her group. I ended up talking to her about the military and other life experiences.

It is December, so we have five more months to complete our tour in Iraq. We have missions daily, searching homes looking for weapon caches. It gets repetitive and sometimes sad. It weird because you can't do anything about it. We are either stuck inside the base or out on a mission. You aren't free to just go anywhere because it is dangerous. Somethings you have to be prepared for. We had missions where we were exposed, where there was sniper fire and we had to take cover. Other times I would hear IED explosions. It is loud and even though you are a klick away from an explosion you can feel the ringing of the explosion. Even though you have Kevlar helmets the ringing gets into your head. You get a migraine feeling, but you get used to it. Other friends of mine died and I get pissed about it. Especially, because there is nothing I can do about it. It is sad. I am in Ar-Rutba with my job to do. Everyone has their good days and bad days. With even the toughest guys in Recon, you can see it on their faces, that the war is taking a toll and that they are tired of the killing. The war wears on you mentally but you must stay mentally strong. So, at this point, I am thinking to myself of things that I would like to be doing back home. You need to understand what a big sacrifice it is to be there and there is something bigger out there than you. I thought I was back in Chicago at one point, because you get used to bullets flying across your head.

My trip to the Syrian border took four weeks and I loved every minute of it. Every day was different and challenging. I got to see people living completely different ways of life. I had a sense of accomplishing something with a group of great men. All of returned from the mission with no casualties.

So, we are back on base. It is Super Bowl time, the Bears versus the Indianapolis Colts. Peyton Manning is my favorite quarterback, even though I am from Chicago. I have a lot of money bet on the Colts to win the game. Peyton Manning was so humble no matter how successful he got. It is 3:30 in the morning our time when we are all watching the game. I am betting against most of the other people. I am watching the game and I see Devin Hester runs back the kickoff 92 yards for a Bear's touchdown in the first fourteen seconds. I upped my bets. The final score was Indianapolis 27, Bears 17. It was a big win for me.

After that there were more missions and building up the base. We helped a lot of folks in Ar–Rutba improve the conditions in the area. In March, we are dealing with people and their attitudes. I tried to be cheery and bust on people, telling them jokes to keep up morale. I seemed to be good at that. We did a joint task force with a Marine Expeditionary Unit("MEU"). The men from the MEU arrive on a Naval ship. We do several joint missions with the men that arrived. We received a citation for the contribution we made to the war in Ar–Rutba.

Reflecting back, this was a significant time in my life where I felt I achieved something. I was able to deal with my demons and angels. As a Marine, we always respected the bodies of the enemies and treated their bodies the same way we treated the bodies of our own soldiers who died. Many times, I had to sleep by dead bodies of both our soldiers and enemy fighters to make sure they were kept safe from the environment around us. We treated people with respect where we could in a time of war.

It is a fascinating thing seeing what you can contribute to life. I totally believe in teamwork. We succeeded and completed the mission at hand which was to make Ar-Rutba better place. There were only thirty of us in Ar-Rutba, but we accomplished a lot. I am a firm believer that you can get any job done, no matter what people tell you, with teamwork. The team can help you get your mind off the difficult tasks and situations you are put in. Sometimes you can forget you are in a war zone.

We worked with Iraqis and watched them go about their daily business while we stayed in Ar-Rutba. I got used to hearing the calls to prayer. You couldn't tell the difference between these people and the people we were fighting against.

In early March, we received orders to go back down to our area of operation in Fallujah. So, we had to pack up again and get ready for the long drive. I was looking forward to seeing old friends and brothers. So, the 3rd recon was out of here.

On the way back to the AO in Fallujah, our battalion had to cross the Euphrates River. As our convoy was on the bridge we took on enemy fire. People don't know what a real shootout is. I was on one side of the Euphrates river and it suddenly went from daylight to darkness. It was like Star Wars. All you see is red flames and you can hear and see the rounds going back and forth, back and forth, and back and forth across the river. It is a crazy feeling, but you get used to it.

We made it back to our marine base in Fallujah. I think we all had the feeling of accomplishment. I thought a lot of us kids became men on the mission. The transformation was amazing. Completing the mission as part of a team was the greatest feeling of my life. My trip to the Syrian border took four weeks and I loved every minute of it. Every day was different and challenging. I got to see people living completely different ways of life. I had a sense of accomplishing something with a group of great men who all respected each other. All of us returned from the mission with no casualties. Thank you 3rd Recon.

Chapter 10

When we arrived back in Fallujah, we received all kinds of kudos for our work further west near the Syrian border. It felt great going through the gates and getting pulled aside by the Company Commanders to tell me what a good job I had done. There were lots of pats on the back and people saying welcome home. We had completed our mission admirably. I was happy to see the others and most of all my friend Auturo.

We had to offload the vehicles and get ready to go back to our barracks. Our barracks were really a big ass trailer park in the desert. Before we left for the mission, I had an unkempt nasty roommate who I had to kick out. You really need to make sure you keep your body and space as clean and neat as you can, especially when you are out on a mission. It is something most Marines pride themselves on.

Things can deteriorate pretty quickly if you let them go and can result in a lot of unnecessary arguments. This time I found a place just for myself.

The next couple of weeks were slow. There were only two to three weeks left in our tour in Iraq. There were very few missions, so we just had basic duty chores. When it is slow, we played a lot of cards. I know how to play, but I don't have the patience to sit at a table. I try to bet big and win big which is usually not the best strategy. The last week, the group decides to have a big poker tournament. There was a $600 buy in, if you wanted to play. There were about twenty people in the whole tournament.

My friend, Auturo, is a great poker player so I decided it was a better bet to fund part of his buy in rather than play myself. I know my limitations. Auturo has an amazing amount of patience. Among the other players was a Sergeant Black, who was part of the 3rd Recon Division who I knew. He was a great sergeant and really cool. The tournament lasted eight hours. Sgt. Black and Auturo were the final two players. I had gone to sleep and returned in the morning to see how they were doing. When I saw Auturo, he said, "I won". My response was "how much did I win". We shared the pot. I was really proud of Arturo. It was a cool experience.

We had to get ready to go back to Kuwait from our area of operation in Fallujah. When we get to Kuwait, we just hang out in Kuwait watching all the people come and go. We were doing pretty much what we were doing back river side. River side means, the place you were detached from. We were winding down, eating food and talking to each other about what we had been through. We really don't talk about much. It usually just talking shit to each other, or saying things like, "I can't wait until I get back" or, "have you seen the new Michael Jordan's basketball shoes that just came out".

The next week we head back to Okinawa. We get on the airplane. We are greeted by the flight attendants. They are giving us the thumbs up and serving us drinks. I didn't really want to drink. After eight and a half months in the desert where there is no alcohol, I didn't feel like getting drunk. Marines often got packages from with liquor in them while we were in combat. People would ask me why I didn't drink. Why would you want to drink in a combat zone? That was not my thing. People did drink and were selling bottles of Scope mixed with vodka for $500.00. You had to be alert and careful all the time. I took precaution and did not drink. So, the Marines are all on the airplane getting drunk and having fun.

Our flight back to Okinawa took almost twenty-four hours. We stopped a couple of times. We flew over Korea. One of the stops was at a small airport in Alaska. It was eleven o'clock at night and the sun was still up. They would not let us get any food. Our company commander started going off on us. We were just trying to eat and pay for our food. They did not want us walking around the airport with our weapons. Here we were just back from fighting for our country in Iraq and they won't let us get something to eat at the airport. It was just crazy. We get back on the plane and touched down in Okinawa at night. The whole third Marine division was waiting for us on the tarmac welcoming us back.

While we were in Iraq our things were put in storage. We had to move to different barracks when we returned. Some of us were smart and ordered some clothes from the East Bay sporting good catalog so they would be waiting for us when we got back to Okinawa, so we could go out that night. After two hours we were ready to go out for the night in order to kick back with some of our friends and have fun for the next two days. Arturo hadn't ordered anything. I had about six jogging suits waiting along with some pairs of Jordan's. We liked the same stuff, so I gave him some of my stuff to wear. We thought we looked hot in our new civvies. I still talk to Arturo often to this day. He has interesting perspectives on the Marines and life in general. He is one of the few people who understands me.

We went back to Kintown to see our homegirls. One of my friend's uncle was president of a Japanese Company. They were well off and took me to a lot of places. I went to Tokyo a couple of times on the weekends. I was living the celebrity life with them. I made great friends. They were a blessing during my time in Japan.

Spring is typhoon season in Japan. Our base got hit by a typhoon and there was water everywhere. We were confined to quarters. Many Marines bought liquor in to their quarters to sit out the typhoon. Some guys got crazy and went out swimming in the water that was about three feet high around the camp. Fortunately, in the end, no one was hurt.

Everything was going well in Okinawa. The battalion was doing great. We are hitting all our numbers. Of course, we were all remembering the friends who got injured and died in combat and some of the traumatic things we had been through. We didn't talk much about it. We went through a lot of debriefings in Okinawa. We had been back for a week, when I became the barracks manager. I was responsible for overseeing the facilities for over 200

Marines. Everything had to be waxed and shiny and the Marines had to have everything in place.

I did regular inspections and started to notice that certain things were out of whack. I found a lot of bibles with holes cut out to hold vials and needles. I never knew that a lot of Marines were using steroids. Most of us just did our work and drank alcohol. I found it hard to understand why these well-trained, in shape guys would use steroids. The ones I talked to thought it was cool and competed with each other on who was better built. I did not think that was good for your body. I did not report anyone. One of the first things you learn in the ghetto was not to snitch on anybody. I would tell the people it is your life and you can do what you want with your body, but I just saved your ass. They would try to thank me and take me out to repay me for not reporting them, but I wasn't having it. Everybody has some types of flaws or addictions, especially after you see traumatic events and go through warfare.

I took the barracks from being 20% compliant to 100% compliant with the Marine regulations. I had to attend a lot of meetings and learn the fire code. I had sort of a skate life, meaning the work was not too hard. I had to perform daily inspections and make sure everything was up to code. I had to report to the Captain and other higher ups. I kept everything at 100%.

Now fall is approaching and we hear that we were going back to Iraq. Some of my friends were leaving and some were staying. I wanted to stay in the 3rd Recon and go back to Iraq with the many friends I had made. My command was pushing for me to stay with Recon. I was supposed to become an NCO a couple of months later. I was told that because I was picking up rank I had to go to another duty station in North Carolina. I was in Okinawa two years and had a hard time saying goodbye to my friends. It was a great life experience to go live in a different country and meet the people. The common curtesy and respect that Japanese people show each other is something many Americans could learn from. The Japanese children are taught how to treat people with respect from a very early age and it stays with them through their adulthood. Okinawa is only seventy miles long. It is a beautiful place to visit mostly because of the people that live there.

We had a huge going-away party, and everybody told stories about me and the others. I got some plaques and awards. I boarded the plane to Chicago intoxicated. The whole trip I am thinking that I wished I could have stayed with my brothers. It is common that you are moved from place to place doing whatever the Marine Corps wants you to do. Unfortunately, when you build a bond with someone, there is always a time it has to be broken. That is what has happened to me, most of my life, so far.

Chapter 11

I arrived in Chicago from Okinawa. I had about a week and a half of leave before I would go to North Carolina. I am glad to see my parents. I wanted to spend time with my wife, Courtney and my son Justin. We hung out and did normal family stuff. I took Courtney to the Military Ball in Chicago on November 11. There were several recruiters there, that I knew from before I became a Marine, Master Gun, Thompson, and Philips. Some had a much higher rank than I did. I respected them all because they treated me with respect. They always gave me the straight story and did not "sell" me to enlist in the Marines. Everyone was in their dress blues. I was not able to go to the 3rd Recon ball because I had to leave for North Carolina. We ate and drank and watched people get awards for recruiting.

I was getting ready to leave Chicago for North Carolina. I went out for drinks the last night with friends and had too much to drink. I was still drunk in the morning. My father had agreed to drive east with me. I got in the car and woke up several hours later when we were in Pennsylvania. He said, it was my turn to drive.

On our way we stopped by to visit Holly's mother and father, who were in their eighties and living in Englewood, New Jersey. I hadn't seen them in a couple of years. I remember the first time I saw Holly's father during the first few months I was with the O'Connors. He was sitting in his home office in New Jersey. I ran up to him and sat on his lap and called him, grandpa. He had kind of a shocked look on his face. He originally thought Holly and Paul were crazy for taking in foster children. Later, he understood and enjoyed telling people he had black grandchildren to see how they would react. That was the last time Paul and I saw him, because he died a month later. Holly's mom is now turning 90 and is still an artist doing a lot of great art work.

I dropped Paul off at an airport in Maryland, so he could return home to Chicago. I took off for South Carolina and did some sightseeing along the way. I stopped to visit UNC at Chapel Hill and Duke. I loved UNC, not only because it was Michael

Jordan's College, I also liked the blue and white colors and was a fan of Dean Smith. My second favorite team was Duke, because they were always a great team. I like Mike Krzyzewski and knew his niece.

When I was in Chapel Hill, I looked at my watch and realized that I only had a few hours to get to the base in North Carolina. I had driven pretty far west from where I was supposed to be going so I headed east. I had to drive east through all of these small towns. Having lived most of my life in or near a big city, it was surprising to me that every fifteen minutes I would be in a new town. As I am heading into Cherry Point, I have to stop to get my papers in order and change into my dress greens uniform. Dress greens are so uncomfortable. I arrived, and someone was there to show me around. It turns out I ended up being at the wrong duty station for about two weeks. Finally, the paperwork gets straightened out and I get to the proper duty station to start training to go back to Iraq.

I am enjoying getting back to training and watching the good side of things going on at Cherry Point. I felt that I was a little bit ahead of my peers as far as training and because I had been in full blown combat in Iraq. Also, the training was better in my 3rd Recon Group. The missions and training exercises we had at Cherry Point were easier and less complicated that the ones I had in San Diego. In San Diego, tactics like escalation of force and de-escalation of force were dealt with in a more formal way and everyone in the battalion was all on the same page. The Marines from Cherry Point I trained with were from the Airwing. They were based in Al Asad, Iraq. We always thought that they had it much easier than the Marines in Fallujah, where alarms are going off and people are blowing up and dying every day.

We continued training and are given new weapons. We are learning to put together a new type of flak jacket which is designed to protect you from shrapnel and other military debris from grenades or other explosives. You wear it over your armor. The older flak jackets just slipped over your head. The newer ones we received in South Carolina are more complicated but protect you better. The final weeks we are going through more classes, obstacle training and other drills. A lot of it I already knew. I had a lot of confidence in myself because of my experiences. I know if you make one mistake it could cost Marine lives or the lives of others nearby.

One day we were learning how to breach an area to minimalize casualties. I explained the methods we had learned in 3rd Recon for breaching.

They asked me about driving trucks and convoys, but I explained there were different rules and tactics for different areas of Iraq because of the differences in terrain, weather and types of enemy violence. I teach them how to properly upload and offload of the vehicles so that they are not picked off by the enemy. Teaching them was so different because they had no idea what they were getting into. There was a lot of laughing and making jokes. They were looking forward to the hazardous pay levels. They hadn't seen the death and destruction themselves. I enjoyed teaching and working with the few guys who wanted to learn and really cared. There were also those that I wouldn't feel comfortable going into battle with.

We start our final packing to leave. I had to redo a will and go over it with the JAG lawyers. I went through all the shots again which made me feel sick. Everything seems kind of depressing and gloomy as we get ready to go to the flight deck to take off. We are up at three o'clock in the morning that day. First, we had to go to the armory to get our weapons to take along on our trip. We do not carry weapons on the base. We had to make sure that the weapons were functional and work with the ammunition.

All the kids with me were laughing and playing around. They had no idea what they were getting into. They think they are going on vacation.

I am talking to some friends about having to go back. It was different this time knowing what I was getting into. I did not trust the people I was going to go back with. They were Marines, but they were goofier and did not pay attention to details. The men were not as professional as the first group of soldiers I went to Iraq with. We are on the tarmac until 4:30. The first flight is ready to take off between 6:00 and 6:30. All the gear is packed. The first group boards. At 07:30 about 15 of us were told we are on standby. This is not a normal standby. Usually we are just waiting for the next plane. We had already said goodbye to wives and family. It turned out we were going to be on a day to day call. It totally surprises us and all our expectations. We got told we are going to stay and we are pissed beyond belief. We had to return our weapons to the armory. After a couple of days, we are still on standby. One week turns into three and we are doing nothing. This was just crazy. Three weeks turn into a month. We are not able to leave the base.

During the wait time I decided to take care of myself and go see the doctor about my foot which hurt most of the time. I just dealt with the pain. I had plantar fasciitis. The doctor shot my foot up with cortisone. Cortisone does not cure anything. It just makes you feel better for a period of time. The doctor also observed that my ligaments were spread apart and told me that I needed additional surgery. I told the doctor I was on standby and we were coming into the second month of being on standby. They said I need to have surgery in June. I was angry and physically drained from waiting. We were just told to take it. It was hard to respect the people in the battalion. I could have had surgery in Iraq, but I wanted to suck it up and stay with the people in the battalion. I get ready to get foot surgery in June. I give the paperwork to the squadron leader to take it to S1. I was given 30 days convalescence leave for after surgery. The paperwork was signed by the doctor and given to squadron personnel.

They gave me Vicodin and Percocet before the surgery for the pain. Corporal Billiard gave me a ride to surgery. I had the surgery and they gave me morphine while I was in recovery. When I woke up, I felt great because of the drugs. I tried to get up out of bed. I put one foot on the floor and fell flat on my face. The nursed laughed at me. Corporal Billiard dropped me off at my car. I shouldn't have driven a car, but I arrived home to my rented house in North Carolina without incident, after stopping for a Slushy. As I got out of the car I tripped and had to crawl up the stairs to my house. The pain was excruciating. I felt like a cripple. I did not know how to use the crutches, so what was the point of having them. I got inside and grabbed a Pepsi out of the refrigerator. I took a couple of sips and passed out on the floor.

Joel C Riley – Holly L O'Connor

Chapter 12

My son's birthday was in a couple of days and since I was on convalescence leave I decided to fly to Chicago to see my son and my wife. I arrived home and I learned how to use the crutches because I was still not able to walk.

I am at home in Chicago and my parents receive a call from a Major at Cherry Point saying that Sergeant Meo was looking for me. Paul came to Courtney's apartment to tell me that Sergeant Meo was looking for me and told me the Major who called had said some bad things about me. I was quite upset at that. When I called Sergeant Meo I argued with him on the phone, which I should have known was disrespectful.

Paul took the telephone call at home from the Marines. The major was rude and told Paul that "Joel was a bad Marine". Paul was furious at hearing that after Joel had served in Iraq and had been retrained, cleared and been on the flight deck packed up and ready to go back to Iraq when he was put on Standby. After Joel had his surgery he could hardly walk even with the crutches.

A friend booked me a flight to leave Chicago in a couple of days. Corporal Billiard picked me up at the airport and took me to my car. I drove to my house that evening because I had a doctor's appointment in the morning which was away from the base. I was going to return to the base after the doctor's appointment. The doctor's appointment was to discuss additional surgery I needed, because I had cysts in my knee. We scheduled the surgery for September. I still had the cast and walking boot on my foot from the first surgery. The doctor gave me Percocet for my pain. As I am getting out of the doctor's office, I get a call from Corporal Billiard telling me to come to his place and turn in my weapon. This is when things started to go very badly.

I drive to Corporal Billiards place. When I get there, another Sergeant picks me up to take me to the base. When we get to the base, military police with rifles open the car door, grab me, force me down into the dirt, and handcuff me. I am angry and yelling because they are hurting my bad leg and foot still in the cast and walking boot. I cannot understand why they are doing this to me. I am embarrassed and extremely angry for the way they are treating me. I was never treated this way in all my time in the Marines. I was taken and thrown into the brig. I was also taken to see the Major that spoke so disrespectfully to my father on the telephone. When I was talking to her, I kept fidgeting because the pain medication was wearing off and my foot was hurting. To relieve the pain, I put my foot on her desk. She took it as a sign of complete disrespect. I should have asked her if it was okay before I did it. She started berating me. I was disrespectful to other senior officers, because I was not able to hold my tongue. I said off hand to one of my friends that a certain major was on my shooting list. I did not intend to hurt anyone or do something stupid like that. I thought I was venting my frustrations to a friend who would never pass it along as if I really meant it.

I am sitting in the brig for about 30 days. I am told by the JAG attorneys that the only way I can get out of the brig was through a Court Martial. I got screwed because I am not familiar with military law and didn't understand all that I am told. The attorney who speaks to me does not tell me the choices I had or explain to me a could get an attorney to properly represent me. My father, Paul, made a trip down to Cherry Point to see me and offered to get me an attorney. I am so angry and frustrated with the Marines at the time, I don't listen to him. I cannot believe that they busted me down to an E1. I have a family and there were bills to pay. A Captain told me I could finish out my service with the military. There is a written summary of what he told me in my military files. I was due to get out in several months. I believed him. They told me several lies in the process, like I could finish out my service and I could get upgraded after I got out. Unfortunately, not having a college education or law degree, I believed what they were saying and signed paperwork which said something different. At that point I just wanted to go home. I thought what I was doing was right at the time. I did not realize how much it would affect me and fuck me up later in life, which it truly did.

I thought brigs were mostly for violent or dangerous people. What I was accused of was absence without leave and several counts of insubordination, which was a verbal indication of my anger and frustration with the way I was treated. In my mind, I was just speaking the truth about the situation. Other people did not listen or like what I had to say, but it was the truth. I was scheduled to have surgery on my knee in September. The doctors determined that I had baker cysts in my knees. My body was breaking down further. I was on house restriction for 60 days. The medical doctor who did the surgery said I should be able to get a medical discharge because of my foot and knee surgery. The military personnel refused to wait for the paperwork. They just wanted me out and not pay me the benefits I was due. I came into the Marines at 100% and worked hard. I came out angry and broken. I felt like I was shit on. I know I am not the only person who feels that way. I want to make sure that others know what they are getting into, because based on my experience the military does not care what happens to their people after their service to the country.

After hearing about the potential Court Martial Paul flew down to Cherry Point, North Carolina and begged him to fight back. They sat and cried for hours, but Joel was so angry and traumatized by the way he was treated, he just wanted out and would not take any advice or help from Paul.

I learned to take the good with the bad. I had to learn it. I do things on a different scale and better understand the difference in types of people and how to deal with them. I realize how difficult life is and try to make things better not worse. The military is not dealing with the problems they create. Others have had it worse than I do. So many men have committed suicide when coming home. Sometimes I wished I did not come home alive and I am sure there are many others out there who feel the same way. Sports players and actors make millions of dollars. The armed service people often give their lives, even if they are still living. The effect of military service on families and friends is enormous. None of us is the same when we return from war.

Chapter 13

I had no idea how hard it would be mentally after I left the Marines. I am out February 9th, 2009. The end of my contract would have been in April. I thought that it was cheap and cowardly of them not to let me finish my contract, since I had been in combat and was completely broken mentally. At that time the Marines did not test for PTSD at the time of discharge. I believe it is required now. I also believe that they forced certain Marines out early to save costs. Someone said they we were held off returning to Iraq because there were too many E-3 rank people set to go and the new Marines were cheaper.

I still have a house I am renting in North Carolina which I had until April. I stuck around for a few weeks to try and get my head together before returning to Chicago to my wife and son. I start to realize how screwed I am by getting an Other-Than-

Honorable discharge from the Marines. I received no benefits at all from the Marines, no education money, no health insurance, nothing. Nobody wants to hire you. You cannot get a government job or join a police force which is a logical progression from the Marines. I had a lot of skills and experience. In the Marines we are vigorous and know how to get the job done without making excuses. We treat people with respect and teach others along the way.

The only job I could get was working security. It is a very low paying job and I used only about 10% of my brain while I was working. I am just working the job, seeing my friends, and going through the motions. Around this time my brother Daniel received a large workers compensation settlement. He had his foot crushed in a machine while working in a plant. He was kind enough to give me $10,000 from his settlement. I pissed it away in short order. I did nothing useful with it. I am back on the streets of Chicago. A couple of weeks after I get back, a friend of mine was killed on 79th street in Chicago. I just get back from Iraq seeing friends die during combat and ironically my friends were dying on the streets in Chicago. I believe that in the military killing is necessary and death serves a purpose. It does not serve any purpose on the streets of the city unless the safety of the citizens is in question. So, I am back where I started from in the streets.

Usually I work the night shift securing property and construction sites from vandalism. I am supposed to call the police when I see people trespassing or committing a crime. Because of my military training I was often able to hold the suspects until the police got there, without having a gun on me. The police would be surprised when they arrived and ask me how I was able to subdue the suspects. I would tell them that I used the form of mixed martial arts that I learned in the marines that consists of takedowns and strong hold moves, grappling, leg locks, etc. I know how to kill a person without a weapon. I just use less force to detain them. That's why I have trouble respecting the abilities of some of the police officers. I thought at one time I would like to train police personnel, but my type of discharge prevented it.

I could not make a career out of security because it is a lazy job. By lazy job I mean it does not use your brain or physical abilities. A lot of security people do not train or look after their bodies, or appearance. They are not paid to do so. I had various jobs but could not really hold onto anything. Nobody would hire or train me for something where I could use my brain and skills and give me the respect I thought I had earned. I had a terrible weight over my head and was in a weird zone where I didn't know what to do with myself.

Joel had filed for medical benefits from the VA, because as an OTH discharge he was supposed to be covered for medical conditions associated with his Military Service. He receives a letter back from the VA that says, "We decided that your Military Service for the period from May 2, 2005 through February 9, 2009 isn't honorable for VA purposes" He was never told this when he agreed to take a plea to get out of the brig. Paul went along with Joel to the VA. to try to get some benefits for Joel. We knew he had PTSD among other medical problems that needed attention.

It turned out that Joel's Other-Than-Honorable discharge was a type that according to the VA was deemed to be like a Dishonorable discharge because of the way the paperwork was written, calling his discharge a "Bad Conduct" OTH discharge. Personnel at the local Hines VA actually tried to get him some help and spent several hours with Paul and Joel, but they were not allowed to help Joel based on the type of discharge he was given. None of this was told to Joel when he accepted the plea to get out of the brig or when he was discharged.

I did not know what to do with myself. My marriage fell apart. I had gotten comfortable with myself as a trained Marine and was not comfortable back in Chicago. I was in a depressed mood that no one could get me out of. I was back to putting up the *wall* in front of everyone and everything. I never let anyone know what I was thinking to protect myself. The cursed part of me thinks that I was a born hustler. That is what I was good at from as far back as I can remember. I went back into hustling. It was easy to get back into. I knew the people in criminal businesses and dealers on the streets. I put my money and energy back into that area of bad behavior. I actually felt like I was a part of something again and felt better about myself because I was in control. I started stealing again. I mostly resold a lot of what other people stole so in my mind, technically I wasn't stealing.

I was not a block nigger who in the ghetto class system was the lowest level. A block nigger is just someone who stands on the street corner and sells drugs. I was in control and managing several people on the street. I was running a business. I always wanted to be the boss. It was not necessarily about having a lot of money. I treated everyone with respect.

In real life, it doesn't help to treat everyone with respect, especially in the business I was in. Often you get stabbed in the back.

I started drinking more and more every day to kill the pain, which was both mental and physical. The VA wouldn't help. I wanted to drink myself into oblivion. Sometimes I blacked-out and sometimes I did not. I was sick and depressed. I cannot or did not want to see a doctor.

Chapter 14

Some people said I would become great and do something important one day. I think this is because I had guts and was not afraid of speaking to anyone. I am good at sizing up people and situations and give good advice. The advice I give is always decent and level-headed. The problem with me is that I usually know what the right thing is, but I am not able to follow my own advice. I believe the demons keep following me and I have trouble kicking them off my shoulder. They keep whispering the wrong thing in my ear. I continue to make the same mistakes over and over.

I had a number of security jobs. I also tried selling Kirby Vacuums around 2010 and 2011. These are large $2000 vacuums that get sold door to door. They are actually good vacuums. I am a natural salesman and I thought I would give it a try. Sales is like talking and walking to me. You have to believe in the product you are selling. Some people sell with no regard to whether the customer will be happy or not. It was the same way I thought about selling gym shoes. You had to make the customer feel good about themselves and the purchase. You must embrace the customer and uplift his or her spirits.

Nine out of ten people wanted the free carpet cleaning or carpet shampoo they get for having me come. You would go to people's houses and set up the machine. It is a big heavy machine. I liked to meet with the people. They would sometimes pay me a little bit for the cleaning. The one person out of ten that really wanted to buy the product could not afford it. People could buy on credit, but most of the people did not qualify. I liked the job because I was driving and doings the selling on my own. You know where you have to be, and you show up on time. I knew how to get around. One day I was told if I sold three more vacuums, I could become an official sales person from Kirby and go to Florida for a banquet. That did not really inspire me.

I had a lot of elderly clients. You have to treat elderly clients like your grandmother or grandfather. You must speak slowly and explain everything simply. One morning I had an elderly man and woman at 9 a.m. They asked me if this would make an improvement in their house. I told them the vacuum costs a lot of money, but it is really worth it. It vacuums and shampoos your carpet with different attachments. As an aside, do you know the dirtiest place in your house is your bed? Your skin falls off every night and stays in the bed even if you clean your sheets regularly. The skin builds up and attracts dust mites. It can get disgusting and you should be vacuuming your mattress regularly. The couple was appreciative of me cleaning various places in their house. I told them they could pay $2000 or pay $1000 to lease the vacuum. I can give discounts from the $2000, but the discount comes directly out of my commission. They bought the vacuum. My next appointment is at 10 am. It was another elderly couple that bought the vacuum. I had to give them a $200 discount. But I sold my second of the day. The next appointment the woman says she has had a salesperson to her house before but didn't have the money. Now she has the money and definitely wants to buy a vacuum. I am three for three this day. You were supposed to sell three a week. My next appointment was at one. I get there 15 minutes early. At about 1:15, I call my manager to tell her that the customer is not here. She tells me to wait because she thinks they are buyers. I wait until almost two o'clock and leave for my next appointment. About 15 minutes after I left, my manager calls and tells me to turn around to go back to the address of my previous appointment. I tell her I am on my way to my next appointment. I was upset because if people don't show up you lose time and sales. We start arguing and saying we have a situation. I did not like the way she treated me. I decided to leave the company and had to fight for the commissions that were due me.

I wanted to stay in sales. My next job was working selling insurance for American Income Life Insurance. The first day I went to the company I showed up inappropriately dressed. The guy told me to go home and change my clothes and come back tomorrow. I did that. He told me he never thought I would come back. He thought that I was persistent and had guts. So, he offered me a job. Insurance agents earn their money through commissions. No sales, no pay. I thought it would be simple to do. I had to talk on the phone and set up appointments. Then I would drive around and meet with the customers. I liked meeting with the customers. Originally, we were told that we did not have to cold call for clients. Then they wanted me to pay out of my pocket for someone to make the calls. They misrepresented what the job would be. There was no teamwork. Everybody worked for himself which was not a good thing. I started making more and more appointments. I found out that a lot of insurance people lie and sell clients products that they do not need. I did not sell anything that the customers did not need. My manager showed me a trick to make more sales. I was doing well but it wasn't enough for me. I had to put myself back in the security field.

I did security up on the North side working at the Black Ensemble Theater. I got another security job at Dearborn Homes, a housing project on the south side. There were some very interesting people there. I was still bored.

I wanted to get my own place. My parents helped me buy a condo out of foreclosure around 35th street and Lakeshore Drive. My parents and I did a lot of the renovation. It was a two-bedroom condo on the first floor that had been flooded. It smelled badly and was in terrible shape. We had to redo the whole thing. We ripped out all the carpeting and rebuilt some of the walls, floors, and the entire kitchen.

Around that time, I started getting terrible migraines. I wasn't taking care of myself. I was drinking heavily. One day I got a headache that was so bad that I had to close my eyes. When I opened my eyes, blood was coming out of my eyes. I knew something was seriously wrong with me. This was about 2012. I was seriously depressed. My parents realized what bad shape I was in. My mom had written to our state senator and congressmen relatively soon after I got discharged complaining about the way I was treated as a veteran. She and Paul were most upset after Paul had spent days at the VA trying to get medical help for me. U.S. Senator Dick Durban had his staff write to the VA, but he got the same message back from the VA that I did. Not a big surprise. I didn't really want any part of it then, because I was suffering from PTSD and was so angry at the military.

We knew Joel had PTSD when he came home to Chicago. When I looked up the symptoms of PTSD on the web, he had every one of them; nightmares, could not sleep, fidgety, could not focus, feeling more irritable or having outbursts of anger, difficulty concentrating, etc. He still had pain from his surgeries.

I spent a lot of time requesting and going through Joel's' military records. At first Joel only told me briefly what happened. Paul had been down to Cherry Point at the time of Joel's discharge. We really felt that the Marines were doing a severe disserve to Joel, given his physical and mental condition. I made a report of all his records, but I didn't see that sending it in would help given the response from Durban. I also watched a three-part video on YouTube Discharge Upgrade Counselor Training with Kathy Gilberd from the Military Law Task Force of the National Lawyers Guild. It was very informative. She gave examples of how many of the veterans were treated and lied to, that were very consistent with what Joel told us about his treatment. He did not want us to go forward trying to help him. I could see that it upset him even discussing it.

I was in the depression mode and did not want any part of rehashing the mess of leaving the military. Everything is not fair in life. I thought I could tough it out, but I am feeling less than who I really am. My parents were seeing me struggle and saw the difficulties I had with day to day life. They saw me in ways I could not see myself. I am fatigued, and I am drinking way more. I get angry and have mood swings. I do not feel like a person. I have to tell them about the migraines. Then, I get a DUI. I knew I had overdone it and I could have done serious bodily harm or killed someone. I was really stupid. I was more concerned about making myself feel good than thinking about others. It cost me the freedom of driving.

I still have the *wall* up for most people. My mom said, "fake it till you make it". When you have a *wall* sometimes one coat of paint isn't enough. Sometimes you need layers and layers of paint and time to make it come out the right way that you want it. You go through these times thinking you are all alone. You can tell people stories but most of the time people don't understand. The people are often judgmental not understanding where you are coming from. At this time, I am dependent on alcohol to survive. After I got out of jail for the DUI, I took all the liquor I had at my house and broke or poured every bottle down the drain.

My friend Rick who worked at my Condo building told me I needed something to calm me down because I was always hyper. Rick smoked marijuana. Weed was never my thing. I thought all the people who smoked it looked stupid and droopy like cartoon characters. My eyes got red when I got tired without drugs. My mom thought I was smoking weed when I wasn't. Rick got me to experiment with weed and I loved it. I got way too high and ate up all the chocolate I had in the house. Since then, I could not get how to balance the weed and the munchies. I continued smoking the weed because it helped calm me down and helped with the migraines.

Chapter 15

Things start to change. One day I got a terrible migraine. I thought I was going to die. I couldn't breathe, and I called an ambulance. At the hospital the doctors gave me all kinds of tests. They put me in a CAT machine that was reading me up and down. They did not come up with anything.

At this point, I reached out to an old school friend. I knew her cousin from when I was young at Maryville. I always had a crush on her as I was growing up. We started hanging out. Her family was a churchgoing family. I was benefiting from them spiritually. She was also there to help try and keep me from going off track. She was a good friend, but she was very controlling and nagged at me. Her father appeared to me to be controlled by her mother. Her mother dictated their entire relationship. One time when I was at their house, her father came home from work at seven p.m. and looked exhausted. Her mother made him go to church. He didn't seem to mind so much. I think that she tried to treat me the way her mother treated her father.

I was working security at McCormick Place, the big convention center in Chicago. This woman I was dating ended up getting pregnant with my second child, Janae. I did not think I was in a situation to be having a second child. My son, Justin, was around eight and I did not do a very good job fathering him. My ex-wife Courtney took on almost all of the burden. Having a child should make you want to break your back to do more.

I got fired from McCormick place and ended up going back to hustling. I met up with some old friends who were dealing in fraudulent internet transactions. They let me in on what they were doing. I am back to my old philosophy that I need to do what it takes to survive. I am making excuses in my mind that it is okay because the politicians and corporate people do it. This time I recognize that I didn't need it to survive, I just needed it. I could make way more money than working a nine to five job in two hours. I don't condone it now, but I did condone it then. I was obsessed with American Greed on television, I saw of these people get rich and wanted some of it. I didn't really consider that a lot of them end up in jail. I think money is addictive. On the other hand, I know there is a wrong way and a right way to do things.

Things get tricky and complicated with Janae's mother. I knew we could never be in a long-term relationship which made things hard. I was trying to deal with her on a day to day basis, because of the baby, but it was not working. I was rude and didn't think about her feelings. It was a very rough time for her. I apologize to her because I was not able to think straight at the time. We were just opposite people. I did not want anyone controlling me.

That August, Janae was born prematurely. She was in the hospital for a long time. I went to visit and held her in my arms. I realized that she was a blessing and God wanted her to be here. She was a fighter and I knew she would make it. My relationship with Janae's mother was spiraling down. Janae's mother thought I was going to take care of her for the rest of her life. My mother warns young women she knows to think before you have relationships with anyone. Get to know and have a clear understanding of who your partner is and do not expect anything from anyone. She wants women to take control of their bodies and lives. My mom preached protected sex and birth control. Obviously, I did not listen to her.

Just because a man is the father of a child does not give the child's mother the right to control him. The father has to pay child support, but that is not guaranteed especially if the father has no income. I did not promise Janae's mother anything. She chose to have the baby and thought she could make me into something I am not.

Chapter 16

Now it is Janae's first Christmas. She is a blessing and a miracle baby. I know she is going to be a fighter and probably make trouble like me. I am much more protective with my daughter. I know I have been rude and have not treated women with respect. I do not want others to treat her that way. I am the wrong person to have a daughter because I am not always the most considerate person. A lot of times I just kid people to see how they react. I try to make them smile but it is not always taken in the way I meant it. I would kill somebody over my child. That is a warning to anyone dating my daughter.

I never wanted my children to be in the situation that I was in when I was young. I am trying but I am not always able to succeed. I did not meet my birth father, Christopher Riley until just before I went in to the Marines. My foster dad, Paul

O'Connor, is my real dad. My mom and dad get the title. They did not get it by birthing me. They are the reason that I am who I am today. I was already Joel Christopher Riley. With the life lessons that they have taught me they helped me through some of the tough times. Paul gets a standing ovation for being my father for sticking it out with me. It doesn't take blood to make a family. It takes commitment. It takes understanding. It takes courage. It takes helping. It takes sacrifice. It takes patience. It takes a great person from God to deal with me. And that is all I can say. God got me a good one. I know I am a difficult person Monday through Monday.

I forgave my birth father, Christopher Riley. I see him occasionally and let him visit with his grandchildren. I know he does not think I am the person he wants me to be. But, he was not the person I wanted him to be. I do not really have anything to talk to him about. He tries to give me fatherly advice, but I cannot really respect him because he wasn't there when I was growing up.

Janae's mother and I never really see eye to eye. Seeing my children makes me happy and seeing them accomplish things in life is really the only enjoyment I get out of life. That, and gym shoes. It is just that simple. When I am with them it is easy for me to be normal. Sometimes parents use the child as a pawn. Janae's mother is trying to treat me like a marionette, pulling my strings. I know I have to spend time with her or she won't let me see my child. I just want to see my child.

Chapter 17

The next relationship I got into was a little unusual. I had a very good girl friend. One day she was on her cellphone and talking to her mother. It turned out that her mother and I had the same birthday, October 10, and we started talking. The attraction was there from the beginning. She was 21 years older than I was. I was always attracted to older women. When I was 15, I dated a woman who was in college. No, I never told my parents about her.

The relationship with my friend's mother started out smoothly. This attraction put me out of my element and brought out emotional things out of me. Even though she was older she was hyper like me. She was old and trying to act younger. My friends kept asking me how I could date a friend's mom. I was attracted to older women because you did not have to teach them anything. My friend's mom was more interesting than most young girls and was very kind-hearted. I did not feel awkward at all dating her. I thought she cared for me. It was not about material things. I thought if a person willing to give up their last dollar for you, that said something about their character. The more willing someone was to sacrifice for you the more they really cared.

I had my own condo at the time. She came over and I stayed at her house a lot. The migraines returned worse than ever. My demons were back, and I had no control of myself. I still think that I am normal. Normal to me is just functioning. I might have been bipolar. I call it mood ring swings. One minute I am happy and one minute I am sad. I am not really looking after or taking care of myself or anyone else. I am just going through the motions. I am holding back and cannot really vent my anger. My emotions are coming out and my body is not feeling the way I want it to be. I did not want to admit that I had problems. I am trying to keep my composure while still dealing with day to day issues. It gets the best of you sometimes. It is hard times. Just because you see me smiling does not mean everything is alright. This poem sums it up:

"I keep my paint brush with me
Wherever I may go,
In case I need to cover up
So the real me doesn't show..."

by Bettie B. Young

The poem is about a paintbrush that I read when I was young. I have layers to me and as I realize that as you go through life, there are many layers added and sometimes you need to put on a fresh coat and go over it with another coat and another. I never showed anyone all my layers. There are a lot of layers to me. It is hard to be sane when you have a little "click-click" in your brain. There are demons with me every day of my life. Some things are harder to get over with than others.

Chapter 18

I am trying to be as normal as possible when I am around people. Many people tend to irritate me. I have always been able to talk to anyone. I could start a conversation with the president of Dubai or sell air to an air company. I had no fear of rejection in dealing with people. I had also never been afraid to say what I wanted to say. But sometimes now, I hesitate to say what I actually want to say. I am afraid of being re/re. This is short for being retarded in Ebonics. I don't mean mentally retarded (I know today that one should say mentally disabled or mentally challenged). My brain is not working properly. There is a chemical imbalance caused by PTSD which gets into your actual day to day life.

I want people to understand that you can see a person who has been in the Marine Corps. But you cannot see what is really inside of them. You can see their behavior change and see them acting out, but you don't know what the cause of it is. I am dealing with all of these emotions that I don't want to come out. I still try to be who I am, but I am having trouble dealing with anger management. I can take a lot, but if you piss me off sometimes things come out of me that shouldn't. My parents told me that you have to pick and choose your battles. But what happens if the battles pick you and you cannot control yourself.

Now, the reality has set in that I have a chemical imbalance in my brain. I am thinking to myself that I am just retarded. The traumatic experiences that you have been through make you who you are. I never tried to understand why I am the way I am. When people say you are not the same, I just want to blow them off. They don't know what I have been through. I am the same person. My mom thinks part of it is because I eat so poorly and don't take care of myself. I refuse to believe that. I am still just who I was.

My dad and mom knew a counselor that had worked with Miles and Derrick, my brothers, on some of their issues. His name was John. My dad told John that if and when John met with me, that I am the brother with the most problems, but you might not see it because he will never discuss his issues with anyone. The *wall* again. Miles told me that if I was going to see John, I needed to talk openly with him or seeing John wouldn't help me at all.

I decided to take a chance and talk to John. When I told John about my early childhood, he really let me vent things from my childhood that I never told anyone else. We had great conversations. He was intrigued with the stories I told and the way my mind worked. He said I was smart as a CEO and was brilliant. I told him he had to be fucking lying because of the retardation I have in my brain; the world is not ready for me. John told me that God put me in a position to be different than anyone else. Someone asked me if I had anything to contribute to the world. I thought that there was no way I could help society because it is so messed up. We accept the violence, the culture for good or bad. Having the chemical imbalance, I thought it was helpful to have someone to talk to. John was more of a friend and listened to me. We discussed my overall life agenda. He was fascinated that I could seem so normal with all that has happened to me. John has respect for me the way I am.

I realized from talking to John that you don't have to be born into money. You don't have to be rich. You have to be you at the end of the day. I never needed to be rich to be who I was. I think my personality is worth millions. A lot of people fake who they are. I never needed the money and the fame to solidify who I was. I would never change even if I was put on national television. I would have to worry about swearing. I am always going to be Joel Christopher Riley, meaning I am going to be sarcastic. I'll be ignorant. I'll talk shit and I'll make people laugh.

John broke this down for me. I realized I could change a lot of things. I have the power of a spiritual mind that I can accomplish just about anything because of the experiences I have been through. I never had confidence in the world because of the situations that I was placed into. He helped me put things into perspective. I now have more confidence because I know that the only way I can be broken is to die.

Every day, I wake up and see that God gives me breath. I think to myself, why shouldn't I be able to learn something, prosper or do something different. You need to look in the mirror and ask yourself, who am I, to really see who you are. I now look in the mirror and see someone who is strong, intelligent, powerful, cultured, versatile and entertaining. I have all of these good attributes, but I still have all of these demons inside. I am a Libra, so I should be able to balance my life.

People should not judge others by the color of their skin or how they look. See the bad things you did but also see what you have done and the potential greatness inside of you. See what you can accomplish to make the world a better place. Look at yourself from different angles so you can see the real you. I know I am not perfect any way that you look at it, but some things I did were perfect.

God is the one perfect thing in this world. No one is bigger than God and everyone should be able to forgive, because God forgave everyone for their sins. And God gave his life for the world. I walk around understanding and knowing that no one is bigger than God. When you figure that out, your life changes and you have a completely different perspective. It is not about Joel Christopher Riley. It is what God talks to you about. God says that you can do this. Life is bigger than you. This throws people that know me off balance. I have changed more to helping out others, rather than myself.

Chapter 19

So how do you attack thinks from a different perspective without anyone knowing that you have alternate plans. You are smiling and acting normal, but people do not understand the way that you think. I am getting ready to break my relationship with my friend's mom. I take time to think about things and usually things happen for a reason. There are many people I love as a person but am not in love with. My mental state at this time is all over the place. I realized that I needed help.

All these years, Joel thought he never needed anybody and that he could fight his own battles. He should have applied more of what he learned in the Marines to his civilian life, like teamwork. In addition, learning that those around him are there to help. Joel finally broke down and agreed that we could try and do something about his discharge.

I dug out all the paperwork I had collected back when Joel was discharged and made him go through all of it with me. He has a detailed memory and a good recollection of the facts. As we go through all of the paperwork I could see that Joel's description of his previous military service and discharge was consistent. We also have seen pictures of his time in Iraq. After listening to Joel and seeing Kathy Gilbard's video, I understood better how the military operated.

I put Joel's version of what happened into a memo and attached all the pages of his military file as support. Paul used to walk by the John Marshall Law School, Veterans Assistant Program every day when he worked in the city. Paul brought in my packet to John Marshall and explained to them Joel's history. They took some time to read it and later called Joel to tell me that Sidley Austin LLP had agreed to take his case pro bono. I knew from working with them when I was at Arthur Andersen that they are one of the premier law firms in Chicago.

I met with Jackson Garvey from Sidley Austin LLP. Jackson Garvey was a lot younger than I was but very respectful. I could see his determination in getting to the facts. He was honest about the odds of winning the case not being great. Still, he handled everything with the greatest care. I know you do not always win, but my mental state was getting worse and did not expect that to happen. I still have sleepless nights and migraines. I wake up not being able to move my hands. I am still struggling to be myself.

I realized I had to distance myself from a lot of the characters that I was dealing with and use better judgment. In October my girlfriend's and my birthdays came around and I didn't' want to do anything except smoke a blunt and have a bottle of 1800. She went out by herself. Other people told me she was cheating on me, but I couldn't care less. I remember the fun and crazy times with her. Like when I jumped on her car because she wouldn't give me my keys and I got arrested. I told the cop that I would slam the door and bust the window. They took me to jail for that. I have nothing negative to say about her.

I went back to Janae's mother briefly. I was still working 11 days back to back. I ended up with pneumonia and passed out at the job. I called my previous girlfriend and she drove me to the hospital. When I got to the hospital, I had a temperature of 104 degrees. The doctor told me, I had the body of an old man, because I wasn't taking care of myself. He said that if I was going to use marijuana, I should eat it rather than smoke it because my lungs were bad.

Paul and I went to the hospital to see Joel. We heard the doctor tell him he had the body of an old man and should eat rather than smoke his pot, to avoid lung damage. He has not followed the doctor's advice. Joel's older girlfriend was there. We had met before and she seemed to care about Joel. She said all the right things but wasn't able to help him out of his mental and physical mess. Even after listening to the doctor, Joel would not see that he needed to make changes in his life.

Chapter 20

During this time, I met someone who really intrigued me, her name was Chanel. She was quiet but was a lot of fun. We started dating. She lived on the West Side of Chicago. I had been in and out of the West Side, all of my life but did not really know the area where Chanel lived. It was a great area right off the Eisenhower expressway.

Chanel was independent and did not need me. I really needed her. I tried to completely distance myself from previous girlfriends. Some kept trying to contact me and bother Chanel with childish games and texts. I got bored with the way my life was going and what I was doing.

I had to dig down deep and learn to treat people differently, especially women. I have to thank and forgive my birthmother Janice Lott, who made me. I need to learn how to respect women. I can't blame my birthmother for my actions. But, I thought I could still be Joel, the party boy.

So, one night I am out with friends, drinking and smoking. The night before someone had given me an ecstasy pill. It had messed me up. I wasn't feeling well. I didn't want to drink that much. I had two drinks. I knew I had to drive. I still have not learned.

I drive too fast and end up hitting a car in the rear. The engine of the car started on fire. I tried to make sure my friends are okay and away from the car. The State sheriff and the police pull up because I am on the Eisenhower Expressway. I had to go to the washroom. I asked politely, but he said, "No you are going to sit your ass over here". I had my cellphone. I had to call Chanel, because it was her car, to let her know what was going on. I tell her the details. She handles it amazingly well.

The cop comes over and tells me I am being taken into jail for drinking and possession. I had blown into the breathalyzer and was told to stop because I wasn't doing it right because it showed I wasn't intoxicated.

I was thinking, how could I do what I just did, that cost me two years of my life. I made another terrible decision and I would be letting my parents down. I go to jail, for overnight. They take me to the county jail the next day because of the drug charge. I had an ecstasy pill on me. I went to court that day and they gave me 30 days of house arrest. That meant I had to wear an ankle bracelet and be monitored for thirty days. I felt like a slave. The monitor was irritating, and I felt worse because I was suffering from arthritis.

After thirty days, I went back to court and they dismissed the drug case against me. But I still had the DUI pending with the city. I knew I wasn't intoxicated but who is going to believe me because I do the same dumb shit, over and over. Here we go again. So, what did I do. I started to pray that things would change for me. They let me keep my license until the court date. I kept on going back to court every month because the case kept getting extended. After two and a half years they dismissed my case. Things were starting to get better.

Around that time, I talked to Joel occasionally. He was still pretty messed up and I was afraid he was going to commit suicide. He talked about not wanting to wake up in the morning and feeling useless. I called the Veterans Crisis hotline at Hines VA center just outside of Chicago. I called the person in charge whose telephone number was on their internet web site. I got her voicemail. Her voicemail said, if this was an emergency call another number. I called the other number and left a message saying that my son, Joel Riley was an ex-Marine and was in crisis and I didn't know how to help him, and could they please call me as soon as possible. They never returned my call

I told Joel he had to go in person and demand some help. All the politicians and candidates were talking about treating our veterans better and cleaning up the VA. It might help if the VA returned calls to its Crisis Hotline. Maybe they would help him now. It would be better if he had the help years earlier.

I was stilled depressed and talked to my mother. She told me I had to go over to the VA which believe it or not was three blocks from my house. I knew from others that VA would help if I threatened suicide, but I was afraid they would also lock me up. There was a lot of news articles at the time about the high suicide rate of Veterans. I did walk over to the VA. They actually listened and got me into some counseling program.

I have to get it into my head that the liquor doesn't help. When you realize that you will be okay without the alcohol, it is the best feeling you can have. You realize that you have a lot to lose by trying to cover up the pain with alcohol. It was a blessing that God gave me another chance. I had not learned from earlier mistakes. It is about growing up and changing. I still have bad and good thoughts. I realized that the good people around me could see that I could be better and that I was a worthwhile person.

I kept asking my dad all the time, what am I supposed to be and how am I supposed to be. The answer came to me from God telling me that you need to work hard for others, not for myself. I can still be Joel Christopher Riley, but a better version of myself.

You must distance yourself from the wrong people without being judgmental. I cannot hold back other people from doing what they need to do, and they should not hold me back from doing what I need to do. You are not being phony when you do that. You have to figure out who you are and who you are going to be. One should be able to count your real friends on your hand and measure people by what and how and the way they do things, through thick and thin. Always to the right or left, my Marine brothers will be there. This I know. Some of the friends I have had over the years are still there, but some have faded, and some have gone. This is part of life, deciding on who you are best to associate with in order for you to grow and become a better person.

Chapter 21

It took a long time for me to start to figure things out. A lot of the mental and physical anguish I suffered was from keeping things inside of me. Because of the internal anger there were certain situations that I could not deal with. Those bad things that happened just got pushed under and piled up inside of me. I could not deal directly with my problems.

I still have issues, but I am trying to work through them. When you are a child you don't know how to deal with them when you are not loved and do not have people to go home to help you and comfort you. All the energy you have is wasted. All this weight is crushing on me and I still have trouble dealing with life.

A lot of people keep bringing up passed situations and try to make me accountable for them. I just want to leave them in the past. But, I do not know how to do that. I have certain pressure points. I just keep pushing and fighting.

I am in a relationship now with a very good-hearted independent woman, Chanel. She is still with me, even though I smashed up her car. She does not really need me. She is an accountant and has worked for the same company for years. She was married and divorced. She thought she couldn't get pregnant because she had tried to with her ex-husband. It turned out that she could get pregnant. She is responsible, and it is a miracle that she puts up with me sometimes. She is the mother of our beautiful daughter Justice, who delights me every day.

A lot of men say that you do not want your girlfriend or wife to be more successful than you are. They don't want their women to make more money than they do. I realize that there are a lot of women supporting men who you think are very successful. It is hard being with a woman who is better than you and can get along without you. But I think a woman can do anything a man can do and sometimes do it better. That is my personal view.

I realized that I was not the best father to my other two children. I always wanted to be a better dad than my birth dad. It was not hard to be better than he was because he was never there. I should have done more. I want to stay in my children's lives and help them to be better people. Hopefully, they will be able to understand what I went through if they read this book.

Chanel comes from a large family on both her mother's side and her father's side. There are doctors and neurosurgeons among other careers. Everyone is doing something to leave their own mark on history. I have trouble matching up to them. My ego gets in the way sometimes. Adjusting takes time, but I know it is for the best. I have a woman who really cares about me and is helping me to grow. Anything worth having is worth working for.

I recently signed the paperwork with my attorney, Jackson Garvey, to apply for the military discharge upgrade. He and his associates at Sidley Austin LLC were thoughtful and worked amazingly hard putting the case together. I am hoping for but not counting on a good outcome.

A few final notes. I liked to mention a few personal thoughts and theories on the success and failures in life based on what I learned in my life so far. You look back on all the things you hoped to accomplish in life. You sit there and debate whether you made the right choices, or are you in the right position or did you struggle or are you still struggling because you are at a low point in life.

These are the things that go through every human mind every day.

Everything that transpired from my birth until now at my current age of thirty-five everything changed because with time there is growth. No matter what you are doing whether it is positive or negative is a lesson in life. I think some of the things that happened in my life are overlooked as far as achievement. I'm not afraid to achieve I'm more afraid of the success of achievement.

My heart was the purest thing I ever had. I use that now to be the person I am now. Over time I've grown to understand that you have to adjust to life and adjust to things in life. No one wants to admit that they need help because we feel like it's a struggle or burden on other people. This is true whether you are a doctor, policeman, garbageman, work at McDonalds, Wendy's etc. It is not bad to ask for help. Just ask for help from the right people.

It is important who you know and how you know them. Understand that if you are the smartest person in your circle that is not a good thing. You need to hear other opinions. Everyone should have their own opinions and own views. We may disagree but that's okay.

One of my revelations was that if God gave up his life for the world to forgive everybody's sins, I should be the first one to live with no contempt in my heart towards people who did wrong to me. No one can just tell you that. You need to figure it out on your own. My revelation was that there is a bigger purpose out there. I came up with a theory that I want you to win so I can "over win". This means I have no jealousy and no contempt. I want you to do the best you can no matter what it is, and I want you to succeed at it. People may think you are just saying things, but if you do it from the heart, it opens a whole other side to life that is actually purer. This is the real truth that you want somebody to do better than you, so they can succeed. This gives you the self-fulfillment of happiness which comes to you when you don't expect it to.

Everybody has been through trials and tribulations and problems in their families. All of these things make you a stronger person because you have been through it. It can also cripple you. I'll be the first one to say it. Do not keep everything inside. I am not necessarily saying psychologists are the way to go but find someone you trust to vent or help serve as an outlet for your problems. I built a lot of stuff up throughout my life. I was like a can of pop that was shaken up, ready to explode. It was suppressed anger.

Always have your own ideas. I always have some of the dumbest ideas, but I am always thinking. Some of your ideas might make a difference. Don't let anyone tell you that your idea is dumb. Some people get intimidated thinking that others will have better ideas. That's part of life.

Your time will come to show what you are really made of and who you are. Everyone has their own opinion and may judge you wrongly. Be real with yourself and understand who you are. Know that you are worth something no matter what others may think.

A lot of people may not want you to succeed. It is not that life has been set up not to succeed it is your brain. You have to look past the small picture. The small picture is what everybody expects you to do. Looking at test scores and background should not put you into a low percentile of achieving which is going to attach to you forever. You have to dream big and plan for your dreams to come to reality. Some things happen in life that you have no control over, especially when you are a child. There is not always going to be a positive outcome. But stick to your script meaning stick to your values, your morals, etc.

But at the end of the day, race does not matter whether you are white, black, Asian, African, etc. We all bleed the same blood. No one is greater than anyone else. Racism and prejudice will always exist. You can't ignore it. I won't go back to those days where I have to be belligerent and ignorant just to get a point across.

Now at 35, I understand myself more than I ever did. I still have a lot of growing to do. I am looking forward to it. It is more of a positive message now. I'm living proof. I am the same person I have always been, over my life history, but I have grown tremendously from all of my experiences, good and bad. I always tell people that a negative plus a negative is a positive. Never count yourself out. Everyone that met me can testify that I never change the beat on the type of person I was, whether I was belligerent, ignorant, loud, obnoxious or too hyper. Some people respected me, some did not. I never felt like I had to disrespect or belittle people because of who I am.

What is important to me now is helping others and seeing a smile out of everyone else when what I am doing comes from my heart. Those smiles are the highlight of my life besides watching my kids grow up and collecting Nikes. Whether you believe it or not I, I am here to tell you that life is real.

In life can go anywhere you want to go. In struggle and hard work there is pain that comes along with it. Going through pain is not easy but you learn from it. Some of us were born poor and some of us were born with money. But money is nothing but paper. It doesn't allow you to have less respect for others. Treat everyone fairly even if life has not been fair to you. Decide how you are going to leave the world a better place than it was when you came into it. Never give up no matter how hard the struggle is.

Thank you to all for reading my story. It helped me to put down some of my life on paper and I hope others will persevere and learn from my mistakes and be able to see the light at the end of the day. I look forward to meeting many people in the future and learning and growing through the next part of my life. Lookout for the life of Joel Riley, Part II. I have no idea how things will turn out, but I have taken down at least part of the *wall* and I am willing to let others in.

*****

About the co-author

Holly O'Connor lives in Chicago with her husband, Paul. She is a CPA and an MBA. Holly and Paul have fostered three boys. This is her first book.

*****